RECLAIMING SPIRITUALITY

Blackwells,
Oxford
13/9/99.

RECLAIMING SPIRITUALITY

A new spiritual framework for today's world

Diarmuid Ó Murchú MSC

Gill & Macmillan

Gill & Macmillan Ltd
Goldenbridge
Dublin 8
with associated companies throughout the world

0 7171 2630 7

Index compiled by Helen Litton
Print origination by Kenneth Burnley, Wirral, Cheshire.
Printed by ColourBooks Ltd, Dublin

A catalogue record is available for this book from the British Library.

5   4

Contents

*In profound gratitude, I dedicate this book
to the loving memory of my parents*

JOHN AND MARGARET

*whose simple faith and sublime wisdom
continue to nurture my spirituality*

Introduction

The theology which undergirded our spirituality in the past cannot be resuscitated and intelligent people cannot live a spirituality which is theologically bootless. We are, to a large extent, running on theological empty.

Sandra M. Schneiders

This is not a balanced essay, for balance often qualifies insight out of existence.

Sallie McFague

OUR SPIRITUAL STORY as a human species is at least 70,000 years old; by comparison, the formal religions have existed for a mere 4,500 years. At the outset, therefore, I wish to establish the centrally important distinction between spirituality and religion. The latter refers to those formally institutionalised structures, rituals and beliefs which belong to one or other of the official religious systems, which include Hinduism, Buddhism,[1] Judaism, Christianity, Islam, Sikhism, etc. Spirituality concerns an ancient and primal search for meaning that is as old as humanity itself and, as I shall illustrate in subsequent pages, belongs – as an inherent energy – to the evolutionary unfolding of creation itself.

Spirituality tends to be perceived as a sub-system or offshoot of formal religion. In practice the reality is quite different. David Hay (1996, p. 293) claims that 'Two-thirds of adults have a personal spirituality, but fewer than one in ten people bother to go to church regularly.' Spirituality is, and always has been, more central to human experience than religion, a fact that is borne out in the growing body of knowledge accumulated by cultural anthropology and the history of religious ideas.

My goal in writing this book is to retrieve the long-lost, subverted tradition of spirituality, and to re-establish its primary significance in the human search for meaning and purpose in life. While our world continues to struggle with religious fanaticism (e.g. fundamentalism in many guises) on the one hand, and religious indifference (especially in the West) on the other, spirituality explodes with new vision and with fresh possibilities for a more integrated world-view.

The religious, moral and spiritual breakdown of our time has to do with religion and not with spirituality. In one sense, spirituality is thriving today and the spiritual seekers of our time know they are on to something worth fighting for. The problem is that they are often misjudged, rebutted and rejected by the propagators of formal religion who – in many cases – are unable to comprehend what is really happening.

Spirituality at a new threshold

This new upsurge of spirituality is itself one manifestation of a world undergoing global transformation on a scale not known to humanity for many millennia. Once again, the so-called educated of our age, locked into the closed-system thinking of the West, fail to grasp the real issues, or name them in a creative way. We fall back on the divisive dualisms that have reaped so much havoc in our world and come up with a set of new ones such as pre-modern and post-modern, pre-Christian and post-Christian, pre-patriarchal and post-patriarchal.

It is fashionable these days to talk about post-modernism (more on this topic in Bertens, 1995). It gives the impression that we are really in touch with something new and important. In a sense we are, but its challenge eludes us while we retain a dualistic world-view. It is becoming painfully clear that dualistic thinking continues to divide and fragment our world when the millions who are spiritually starving yearn for peace and unity.

At this moment in our evolutionary story as a human and planetary species, where we stand in terms of pre- or post- is of no real significance. Much more helpful and enlightening, I suggest, is to take seriously our evolutionary unfolding which is about transcending what existed previously in order to grow into the future that beckons us forth; hence my use of the prefix 'trans' which I will adopt throughout this book.[2]

I use the synonym *trans-patriarchal,* to denote those spiritual desires and movements which seek to outgrow the restrictive and oppressive parameters of patriarchal ordering.[3] Instead I wish to adopt the evolutionary vision that enables us to perceive unfolding rhythms and patterns – across millennia rather than merely in decades or centuries. The spiritual consciousness of our time is not focused on abandoning anything; the deep yearning is to outgrow, transcend, evolve towards the new that is beckoning us forth; hence my preference for the prefix 'trans' rather than 'post'.

The central thesis of this book is that humanity today yearns for a bigger picture than our currently subsumed perceptions which entangle us in webs of religious minimalism. This yearning for the expanded picture is the heart of trans-patriarchal spirituality (see Kelly, 1993 for its application to theology). We yearn to reclaim the deep, primal sacred story of our evolving universe; of planet Earth as our cosmic home; in the diverse and magnificent array of life-forms around us; in the largely untold story of the evolution of spiritual consciousness within humanity itself; and, finally, in the contemporary desire to create a one-world family characterised by love, justice, peace and liberation.

The spiritual landscape we explore is both ancient and new. For us as humans, spirituality is a natural birthright, which over the millennia has been weaving a tapestry of elegance, grandeur and beauty, with the inevitable scars of an evolving universe. At this time of global transition, we need to re-connect with that great tradition and reclaim it afresh in the context of our new evolutionary moment. Could any task be more exciting? Could any be more relevant? And could any be more urgent for the changing times in which we live?

The spiritual hunger of our time

When it comes to religion, many of the most thoughtful young adults are really post-denominational. They want spiritual experience and the ethical responsibility it implies, but they are not committed to the us-versus-them ideology that has accompanied so much of the history of institutional religion.

Matthew Fox

In this realm, there is a new kind of freedom, where it is more rewarding to explore than to reach conclusions, more satisfying to wonder than to know, and more exciting to search than to stay put.

Margaret J. Wheatley

OVER THE PAST TWENTY YEARS, several studies and surveys – in Europe and the USA – indicate changing trends and patterns in religious observance. There is extensive evidence that religious practice is in decline, and amid growing 'secularisation' religion is battling to hold its place in our rapidly changing world.

A number of those same studies indicate that many people who exhibit an interest in – even a curiosity about – religious matters (such as the existence of God, the spiritual meaning of life, etc.) do not necessarily follow, nor abide by, the requirements of formal religious practice. While formal religion seems to be losing its dominant role, there appears to be a growing interest in the things that pertain to religion; hence, the paramount importance of the distinction between religion and spirituality, highlighted in the Introduction. The latter refers to those millions across our world who hunger for deeper meaning and for what we have tended to call 'transcendent values'. The former refers to those who follow one or other formal religion.

This book attempts to unearth the growing spiritual consciousness that is irrupting in our world today, and specifically in the lives of those who have either veered away from (or abandoned) the practice of formal religion, or may never have had a religion in the first place. For many people it is virtually incomprehensible that spiritual yearnings, feelings or values can arise apart from the context of formal belief; in other words, religion is perceived to be the only fountain from which spirituality can spring forth.

Fortunately, human experience suggests otherwise and has done so over many millennia, as we shall indicate in subsequent chapters. It is not a realm of human experience that has been researched or studied systematically as has happened in the case of formal religion. Consequently, we rely on anecdotal evidence, which is now becoming so widespread and compelling that we can't afford to ignore it any more. The following case history – Ian's story – describes dominant features, and one of the many unfolding patterns that characterise the new spiritual awakening. It may be considered a parable for our time.

The pain of being misunderstood

Ian Gaskill felt none too comfortable walking into a vicarage in North London; his parents had advised him to do so since they were unable to answer his probing questions.

Confronting him was a sturdy, red-brick building, shadowing a small gothic church that Ian had never entered in his life. He wondered what type of reception awaited him. True to expectation the vicar was donned in black clerical garb, but the firm handshake and warm smile helped to diffuse a good deal of Ian's fear and anxiety.

'My parents advised me to come and see you . . . there are a number of things about the Church of England that I'm not very clear about. . . .' A versatile and transparent communicator, Ian proceeded to fill in the background. Born into a 'middle-class' British family, neither he, his parents nor his sister ever went to church or practised religion.

'So, what did you do on Sundays?' enquired the vicar.

As far as Ian could remember, back over his twenty-one years of life, Sunday was always a day to explore the forest and woodlands. The whole family went to the woods, often taking a packed lunch with them. There wasn't a tree or shrub in any wood around London that Ian could not name or a chirping bird that he could not identify. Not surprising, therefore, when he entered university in September 1986, he chose to follow a degree course in environmental studies.

Shortly after entering university, Ian joined CND (The Campaign for Nuclear Disarmament), very active at that time, since Mikhail Gorbachev (of the then USSR) and Ronald Reagan (then President of the USA) had not yet signed their first historic agreement to work towards the diminution of nuclear arsenals and inaugurate the end of the Cold War. With typical student idealism, Ian threw himself heart and soul into the work of CND, attending meetings, participating in protests, addressing gatherings. A great deal of external action accompanied by some strange internal stirrings of the heart and imagination aroused questions like: 'Why am I so involved in this organisation?', 'Why am I so preoccupied with protecting and saving the planet?' (In this latter question he often felt as if he was referring to his own body.)

Very active in the same CND group was Alinka, a woman of Indian origin, brought up in the Hindu faith which she no longer practised. Frequently, she spoke of the *sacredness* of the Earth, indeed of creation at large. 'What does she mean by that word *sacred?*' 'What makes something sacred?' became some of Ian's probing questions. Not surprisingly, many an intense dialogue followed between Ian and Alinka.

Then one day, Alinka invited Ian to join her for the weekly session of Buddhist meditation that had become a spiritual anchorage in her life. For Ian, too, it was a landmark of spiritual maturation, an experience that continued to nurture his emerging faith for the remaining three years at college.

Ian's pilgrimage into the world's great faiths took some fascinating twists and turns. One day in the college library as he struggled to put the final touches to a tedious project, his eyes wandered across the great aula, his gaze landing on the young man wearing a turban. 'Now, that means that he is a Sikh! I wonder what do Sikhs believe in?' Well, one way to find out is to go and ask him – initiating a conversation which finished in the college bar about three hours later.

Two years further on, Ian is at home with his family for a weekend break from college. The main evening television news gives extensive coverage to the debate in the Synod of the Church of England on whether or not women should be admitted to priesthood. Ian's curiosity is aroused once more, as this time he seeks to unearth what the Church of England is all about. While his mother gives all the respectful attention she can, she feels unable to answer even his most basic questions and suggests that the vicar down the road is the person he should approach.

Neither Ian, nor his mother, could have foreseen the next development in Ian's emerging spiritual story. The vicar – a man in his late 30s – was quite evangelical and considered Ian's religious meanderings something of a waste of time. As Ian struggled to articulate his questions about 'religion in this country', the vicar interrupted in a somewhat agitated tone: 'Listen, for a moment son, just answer me one question: do you believe in Jesus Christ or do you not?'

'What do you mean . . . I don't understand . . .' Ian racked his confused brain, trying to figure out why Jesus Christ was brought into the conversation so suddenly. Ian sensed that he was on a collision course. A frozen, awkward silence, accompanied by a vacuous glare, suggested that he had 'thrown his pearls in front of swine'. He had not been understood and he sensed he would not be. He said he felt very uncomfortable and, perhaps, should leave the conversation until another time. The vicar agreed; with a sense of relief, it seemed. He offered neither affirmation nor encouragement to Ian, nor did he suggest another time in which they might continue the conversation.

Duty done, with the standard 'Thank you' and 'Goodbye', the bang of the vicarage door cracked open within Ian an overwhelming sense of rage and anger. He drifted into a local park, sat on a bench, felt like crying his heart out, but no tears would come. Everything that was precious and sacred to him had been totally devalued and undermined. He describes the moment as the one and only time in his life (thus far) when he felt totally rejected by another human being. Ironically, the one by whom he felt so rejected claims to be a representative of Jesus Christ!

In the aftermath of that painful experience, Ian came to speak to me after a lecture I had given at an Ecology Conference in London in May, 1989. Although now some months since the talk with the vicar, the emotional and spiritual scars were all too obvious. Fortunately, I was able to offer a listening ear and a non-judgmental heart; I also affirmed him strongly in his story, in his exploration, and in the profound faith that underpinned his spiritual search.

I had a strong sense that things would work out to Ian's advantage, and in due course they did. He met Linda who had read environmental science at another university; they fell in love and eventually married. Linda is a Quaker, a deeply reflective person. Ian and Linda were married in the contemplative stillness of a Quaker Centre; they held their marriage feast in an open field. Today, they both live in an ecological commune in Sweden, working to alleviate the destructive effects of acid rain in that country.

Ian's story deserves to become a prototypical parable for the spiritual hunger that pervades our world today. Millions share this hunger, but relatively few enjoy the fortune of bringing it to fruition as Ian has succeeded in doing. Some can't find even a language or a social context in which to begin naming their reality or telling their story. And some who do, end up terribly damaged and alienated, because like Ian they seek accompaniment from those who are neither equipped for, nor capable of, befriending this unfolding process.

For the remainder of this chapter, I want to unravel some of the central elements of this new spiritual journey, along with its implications for all of us as we move into a new millennium in which spirituality is likely to enjoy a significant revival. People like Ian may well be trail-blazers in a new spiritual revolution, the ramifications of which are likely to be formidable and far-reaching. Let us begin by reviewing some of the key questions that surface from Ian's story:

1. How do we identify and discern signs of spiritual awakening in people like Ian?
2. Are there identifiable stages of spiritual unfolding that happen in the lives of such people?
3. By prioritising spirituality over religion are we witnessing a counter-cultural movement and, if so, what are some of its key elements?

Signs of spiritual awakening

Ian Gaskill is quite an ordinary person, perceived by his parents as a questioner and by his peers as one who takes life 'a bit too seriously'. He has had the good fortune of a very supportive home and a loving family which, despite a total absence of religious belief, lived in a caring and responsible way displaying neither animosity nor disregard for religion. In the environment of Ian's upbringing, religion is considered neither good nor bad, simply irrelevant.

The first outstanding feature of Ian's spiritual development is a keen love for nature. This is deeply ingrained in his family ethos. The Sunday trip to the woods had become a kind of family ritual, a rite of passage, that evoked for Ian a deep spiritual fervour, and a growing awareness that our world is a sacred place imbued with meaning and joy far beyond anything we humans can ever give it.

Secondly, Ian is blessed with a well-developed capacity to think and reflect. Ian was always a questioner and his parents encouraged him to be one. Fortunately, the educational system – which thrives on making people think according to political and cultural expectations – did not succeed in undermining Ian's searching mind and heart. The inability to think deeply and imaginatively is one of the most serious social, cultural and spiritual deprivations of the contemporary world. In the West particularly, we are conditioned into being linear, rational robots, starved of the capacity for imaginative and creative reflection.

A third outstanding feature in Ian's story is his narrative fluency. Ian is proud of his story, in its several dimensions apart from those narrated at the beginning of this chapter. With joy and confidence he tells that story in a very natural way and listens to its unfolding meaning. This is a rare gift in today's world, bombarded as we are with facts, figures, statistics, reports, rational mind-sets and mechanistic modelling, often leaving people bewildered, feeling overwhelmed, succumbing to self-doubt and a debilitating sense of alienation from self, others and the surrounding world. There is little room in our culture for the creative imagination and the liberating power of the story-teller.

Stories liberate possibilities, break down established structures and catalyse the creative imagination to dream alternative ways of doing things. What seems simple and natural is, in fact, quite a sophisticated skill, which despite its great age and abundant usage (Jesus, and all the great religious leaders worked with the medium of story) is poorly understood, largely unappreciated and only marginally integrated into our Western cerebral and rational culture.

Another outstanding feature in Ian's life is his capacity to relate. Again, we are dealing with something that seems very ordinary and basic to human living, but is a good deal more complex when explored in depth. The encounter with the vicar was jeopardised precisely because of the clash of the relational and the patriarchal modes. The vicar, engrossed in his Messiah complex, felt threatened by the story-teller who wants to open up a relationship in which the story could be explored more deeply; the vicar felt compelled to give 'answers' which might be under threat (i.e., proved to be irrelevant) if he allowed the story to unfold at length.

Ian's capacity to relate – which we can assume he inherited largely from a caring and loving family – bequeathed to him a strong sense of trust, intimacy and the capacity for exploration. This is what also saved him from the alienation and ennui that could have so easily destroyed him. Confronted by deep anguish and confusion, Ian did not seek to escape into some hedonistic panacea of alcohol, drugs or gambling. Nor did he try to suppress the darkness that at times must have felt quite overwhelming. He tended to seek out friends or kindred spirits to 'talk things through'. His ultimate reward was a life-giving relationship (with Linda) of tremendous complementarity and affirmation.

Ian's capacity to relate, however, is not just about people, but also about the planet we inhabit. When I first met Ian I was left with the impression of a person in deep despair. When I subsequently shared that perception with Ian, I discovered that I had been quite mistaken. When confronted with so much misunderstanding, I asked him if he ever felt suicidal. 'It never crossed my mind,' he informed me, and went on to say: 'I love the planet too much to abandon her like that.'

What in fact he meant is that he feels so cherished by life, planetary life included, that there was no way he could yield to an act of ultimate abandonment. And this is further confirmed by the option he and Linda made to live in an ecological commune, where love and intimacy are shared, not merely with an extended human family, but within a social and environmental context where befriending creation itself is also a perennial value – and, it would seem, a central tenet of the unfolding spirituality for the new millennium.

The search for authentic community – which the Christian churches hail as their primary goal – is a pervasive aspiration of our time. It is not easily realised in our atomistic, competitive world and tends to be fostered on the margins and liminal places by those who are fired by higher ideals and transformative spiritual vision.

The capacity to relate, which drives some spiritual seekers of our time towards more communal ways of living, seeks to outgrow the boundaries and restrictions which we in the West consider to be

normative and essential. We have created a set of formal structures
– some of which seem to have survived the test of time – such as
monogamous marriage, the nuclear family, the formal workplace,
religious institutions around which we have set definitive and even
dogmatic boundaries. These boundaries translate as laws and regulations by which certain peoples and behaviours are included and
others excluded. Without these boundaries we fear there would be
widespread anarchy, chaos and disintegration. But leaving such
boundaries unquestioned and unexamined – as the Christian
churches suggest when they claim that the family is of divine insi-
titution and shoud not be tampered with – is in itself a prescription
for ultimate disintegration, often preceded by a tragic trail of pain
and oppression.

The capacity to relate is not merely a psychological, social or culturally determined behaviour pattern: it also embodies deep
spiritual aspirations which seek to outgrow several cultural boundaries which we largely take for granted. The desire to outgrow
boundaries is, however, the subconscious dimension of a creative
energy that seeks new horizons as its conscious desire – hence, my
preference for the prefix 'trans' rather than 'pre' or 'post', as
outlined in the Introduction. The spiritual seekers of our time
exhibit an intuitive sense that many old and honoured realities
are no longer meaningful or relevant; they have served their purpose and now need to be consigned to the archives of our sacred
history.

This stance often evokes a panic reaction that fears the demol-
ishing and destruction of everything that belongs to our sacred,
patriarchal tradition. Today's spiritual seekers do not set out to
demolish or destroy anything. They want to give themselves heart
and soul to the emerging new 'horizons', in the course of which the
old may be revitalised on the one hand, or discarded on the other.
This apparent disregard for the old is the one feature of our age that
the guardians of orthodoxy find so hard to comprehend. Correspondingly, because the new spiritual seekers are acting out of a
largely subconscious motivation they find it equally difficult to
explain. This may well prove to be the most daunting but fertile
dialogue that will engage us as we strive to make sense of what is
evolving from within the new spirituality.

Stages of spiritual unfolding

The research of James Fowler (1981, 1984) has proved to be a revolutionary landmark in our understanding of how faith develops in human life. I say revolutionary because it requires a radical reappraisal of the simplistic, linear approach whereby we assumed that faith was 'passed on' from one generation to the next, and that the enculturation of faith was so dependent on God's grace that we could contribute little to the process. On the other hand, most of the religions promote and foster sectarian institutions (e.g. Catholic schools) in order to ensure a solid formation in their respective faith traditions. In the light of Fowler's research we now need to address religious education from a radically new perspective.

Our Christian educational systems (and all the formal religions follow suit) advocate an approach of inculcating a religious sense as early as possible in a person's life, with a view to obtaining formal (and lifelong) commitment by late adolescence and before they leave school. Subconsciously, if not consciously, this approach is quite crudely motivated: get them in before they can think for themselves and begin to question the meaning of things; we need to hold on to them to maintain our presence and impact in the world. Essentially this is a numbers game where quantity and not quality seems to be the central criterion and motivation.

Fowler and other researchers highlight both the futility and danger of this approach. They indicate that faith development in early childhood is quite complex and requires a trusting and supportive environment to be negotiated meaningfully; that the adolescent stage of rebellion and agnosticism is appropriate and even desirable (true faith is about doubt negotiated, not about doubt avoided); that adult integration of faith values and convictions is virtually impossible by late adolescence and belongs much more to the stage of young adulthood (21–35), the stage of Individuative-Reflective Faith; that a mature lifelong faith commitment tends to be a development of the past mid-life (40+) phase, and is often the fruit of a personal crisis, trauma or breakdown.

In Fowler's view (supported by several other researchers), the development of religious faith today does not follow a linear progressive process of gradually expanding understanding and progressively deeper commitment. Integration of genuine faith is essentially an adult attainment, one that can ebb and flow many times before maturing into a more universal ambience in the latter half of life (provided the earlier stages are appropriately negotiated).

Fowler's final stage of universalising faith merits special attention because it is a recurring theme in the spiritual unfolding of many people today and is often accompanied by a strong desire to outgrow and abandon all allegiance to particular religions or to denominational churches. Sometimes, as in the case of Ian, it can be the starting point of spiritual awakening, manifesting in a sense of connectedness with the divine at the heart of creation, or in the perceived sacredness of nature itself.

Fowler's research is aimed at the world of religious belief, related to faith development as it unfolds in the context of formal religion. While his insights and discoveries are immensely significant, they are of limited application to the subject material of this book: the spiritual emergence we are trying to explore. The new spiritual agenda requires a different set of investigative tools. There are no clearly delineated stages, but there are some common experiences which merit special attention, and Fowler's insights and discoveries can help us to unpack their deeper meaning.

1. There is an awakening stage which can be triggered off by a whole range of events or experiences, usually related to questions of meaning or lack of it, in one's daily life. Common experience suggests that there is no conscious religious or spiritual awareness at this stage.

2. This is often followed by a stage of internal confusion, which may also precede the awakening already referred to. People doubt their own experience; might try to suppress it or rationalise it; might seek to explore it secretly; feelings of anger or rage may arise (aimed at oneself, the religious culture, or 'God'). If the confusion persists, it may become deeply disturbing and even disorienting in daily life.

3. Either through one's own initiative, or more commonly under the instigation of peers or friends, an earthing stage may follow. The spiritual seeker decides to join a meditation group, participate in a justice project, do voluntary work in a charitable organisation, have a chat with a priest or vicar, engage in formal worship. This can be a precarious and risky process – 'groping in the dark' – because many people who belong to religious

institutions have neither the intuitive, listening or discerning skills to appreciate and understand what is happening. The perennial temptation will be to offer answers which were designed for questions belonging to another reality, namely the realm of formal religious belief.

What is most bewildering for the contemporary spiritual seeker is the cultural vacuum that often leaves spiritual explorers feeling misunderstood, disillusioned and vulnerable. It is all too easy to fall into the temptation of following the clear-cut answers offered by so many contemporary sects and cults. To provide alternative sacred spaces for the spiritual seekers of our time – with people trained in the appropriate skills of accompaniment and discernment – requires the primary and urgent attention of all people of good will.

4. Depending on how the last stage is negotiated, there will tend to follow a stage of maturing depth and conviction, not based on secure answers, but on questions that continue to unravel the enfolding and unfolding mystery. This tends to be the stage of 'no going back'. The fascination has gripped the heart and soul; something deep within has changed profoundly. The person may not go to church or talk about God, but deep within a transformative experience has taken root, colouring one's entire life-orientation and value appropriation.

5. This tends to have far-reaching consequences, pushing the adherent towards the stage of universalising one's faith experience. One begins to see everything differently, and the fundamental goodness of the benign mystery permeates all creation. Religionists are quick to label this as pantheism or in some 'new age' circles it can manifest as a type of holy carelessness. Its shadow dimension often surfaces in the tendency to deny the pain, suffering and injustice in the world. Instead of the procreative engagement that genuine faith requires there often surfaces a naïve optimism which believes that injustice and suffering will disappear when everybody learns to meditate. Here we encounter the age-old tension between faith and good works, the integration of which continues to be a serious challenge, even for those attracted to the new spirituality.

6. Finally, not once but frequently, there is the stage of coming home to oneself as a spiritual being, sometimes requiring a prolonged struggle to ground one's convictions in a concrete and

practical way. There are several dimensions to this stage and some of the most frequently noted include:

(a) a sense of inner peace, even in troubled times;

(b) a tendency to adopt ethical standards in lifestyle and work;

(c) the development of a spiritual praxis – meditation, prayer, worship, etc. – which may, or may not, include involvement in a formal religion;

(d) the development of strategies to deepen one's spiritual progress (reading, quiet times, etc.);

(e) involvement in cultural or social movements addressing the injustices and wrongs in our world.

The spiritual ferment of our time is too amorphous and volatile to provide (as yet) any clear analysis of how spiritual unfolding happens in the lives of contemporary people. Consequently, the stages outlined above are best regarded as pointers, indicators of what the Creative Spirit (who animates and sustains all spiritual growth) is doing in our world and in its peoples. Taken together they provide different aspects of a complex and creative landscape; not all elements are enumerated here, merely the ones that contemporary experience, thus far, is highlighting on a fairly universal scale.

Spirituality as counter-culture

This new spiritual resurgence is not something planned by a specific group of people or by some new organisation that is seeking to undermine the significance of churches, religions or the culture of traditional faith and belief. This is a proactive rather than a reactive movement. Many of the people involved in this spiritual reawakening have little or no familiarity with formal religion. These people are not anti-religion and should not be confused with those who denounce religion because of some past hurtful or destructive experience.

In fact, we are dealing with a phenomenon that defies human comprehension. We are witnessing a movement of our time motivated or driven by a creative evolutionary force (see Laszlo, 1993) over which we humans have little or no control. We are being carried along by a new surge for meaning, which, contrary to many religious beliefs, is not drawing us away from the world but plunging us more profoundly into it, not alienating us from the divine but re-connecting us with the God who co-creates at the heart of creation. Not surprisingly therefore, the new spiritual search takes on global significance for many of its adherents.

Because of this global impact and ambience, we need to bring new tools of investigation and exploration to this field of research. No one discipline, no matter how sanctioned by time, will enable us to comprehend this new upsurge; it requires a multi-disciplinary analysis. More importantly, it needs to be explored within the paradigmatic shift of consciousness and knowledge that affects every area of investigation today (the approach adopted by Wilber, 1996). For the purposes of this chapter, I draw on one piece of research that seeks to highlight some overall governing factors which, today, impinge upon every sphere of knowledge, and seem to have a particularly significant application to the spiritual upsurge being explored in this book.

I refer to an important piece of research by the American specialist in the study of religion and culture, Stephen Happel (in Russell, Murphy & Isham, 1993, pp. 103–34) who has identified three factors which impact upon every sphere of human and planetary life today: surplus, imbalance and open-ended directionality. All three feature strongly in Ian's story and seem to be significant namings for what is transpiring in the evolving spirituality of our time.

Surplus and the enlarged horizon

Happel borrows the notion of surplus from Paul Riceour's work on how we deal with questions of meaning. In our various attempts to address the questions, we find ourselves drawn into considerations and engagements that push the horizons of understanding beyond every 'here-and-now' reality. We are always drawn into a larger frame of reference, even when we seem to be immersed in the narrow confines of confusion, pain or meaninglessness (as long as we stay with the struggle of trying to make sense of those realities). In this process of unearthing the deeper meaning, we adopt linguistic and symbolic skills to negotiate our pursuit. Chief among these, and of particular interest to both Riceour and Happel, is the use of metaphor (see Riceour, 1967, 1976, 1977).

Metaphors are linguistic devices we use in daily discourse. We speak of something happening 'as quick as lightning'. To say that it happens at a very fast rate fails to captivate or articulate that extra dimension – the surplus – that, on the one hand, seems to defy expression yet is essential to the meaning intended by the speaker.

According to Riceour (1976), we use metaphors to unravel 'the surplus of meaning'. In those many experiences of personal and planetary life, we are frequently dealing with realities which in our rational, cerebral world we think we have grasped and understood fully, but even in the misunderstandings that arise in ordinary conversation we have abundant reminders that the communication of meaning is a complex and intriguing phenomenon. Why? Because we are creatures continually grappling with issues of meaning and always pursuing deeper meaning (the surplus) in every aspect of our lives – usually at a subconscious level.

Our world today yearns to outgrow the stultifying and crippling boundaries with which we have tried to hem in the human search for meaning over the past 300–500 years. This has been an era of mechanistic modelling, patriarchal control and the triumph of rationality. It has reaped many advantages for humankind but has now outgrown its usefulness and is proving not merely irrelevant but highly destructive for the future well-being of person and planet alike.

The 'surplus of meaning' bombarding us in today's world has two dominant orientations. Firstly, a massive reaction against the oppression and repression of the past, manifested in the tendency to throw overboard all structure and institutional reality. What contemporary philosophers call deconstruction serves as a pertinent example: in its literary application it invites us to distrust all language, which it perceives to be loaded with meanings that suit the desires and purposes of the ruling classes. In the realm of human sexuality (explored at length in Chapter 8) we note a tendency to dissolve many of the traditional boundaries relegating sexual behaviour to monogamous marital relationships. Politically and ecclesiastically, fewer and fewer people look to those who govern them for inspiration or guidance; increasing numbers bypass or ignore higher authorities in several areas of contemporary life.

The surplus being addressed here is the shadow side, fuelled by instinctive reaction that no longer wishes to tolerate limiting restrictions, and in the process of 'breaking out', will tend to go overboard in defiance of current norms and expectations. Politically and religiously, such norms are considered to be permanent, unchanging and unassailable; therefore those infringing such standards are labelled deviants.

Many Christians, clergy and lay, would consider Ian Gaskill to be misguided and deluded in seeking spirituality outside the Christian church. They would suggest he was in danger of blurring his faith by dabbling in other religions. Celebrating his wedding in a combination of a Quaker Meeting House and an open field would be considered by many to be an utter abomination. But for Ian and many other spiritual seekers, these are all spontaneous, natural, intuitive responses to the 'surplus of meaning' with which they are striving to engage, and this brings us to the consideration of the second dominant orientation.

The reactive behaviour tends to win public attention and usually public denunciation. We fail to realise that it is positively and not negatively motivated. Ian Gaskill has no intention of offending religious people or of undermining formal religious belief; he is not an anti-religious person. And he sees nothing wrong in trying out a whole range of different faith experiences. The conflict that believers tend to experience strikes him as strange because he does not share those experiences. The priority of Jesus amid Christian believers and the unique nature of Christian revelation are theological concepts that make no sense in Ian's growing spiritual awareness. He may suspect that these are ideological remnants of a previous age – and a substantial proportion of Christians are likely to agree with him!

Ian is challenged and inspired by the 'surplus of meaning' cascading upon our world today, a deep archetypal upsurge that calls us to:

1. reclaim planet Earth (and the entire cosmos), and not just our own country or continent as our primary experience of being at home in creation;
2. outgrow our national, ethnic and religious differences which are human constructs that belong to the patriarchal hegemony of ages past;
3. affiliate afresh with the Earth and with the creative universe as the primary life-force (the great cosmic womb) from which we all receive our life and nourishment;
4. connect anew with our co-evolutionary God who co-creates with all life-forms that inhabit our universe throughout the ages.

Seekers like Ian are prophetic people who seek (often unknowingly) to stretch boundaries and explore possibilities in what they sense is a world of unlimited abundance, with largely unexplored cultural and spiritual resources. Despite their utopian vision, such people tend to be aware of the surpluses that already exist but are portioned out in such a distorted, unjust and oppressive way: wealth, food and economic resources largely controlled by one-third of humanity while the two-thirds world wallows in degradation and starvation. Many people also are aware of the complex political and moral implications of the surplus of overpopulation, stretched to unsustainable limits, reinforcing scarcity and deprivation, already enforced by the grossly unfair distribution of world resources to suit Western political expediency.

Surplus is a central notion in the spiritual and cultural vision of our time. It is inundated with light (enormous potential) and shadow (unprecedented catastrophe) and requires profound wisdom and discernment for a comprehensive assessment. Most important of all, we must not shy away from the challenge it presents: to break open and outgrow the many congealed and closed systems that still prevail in the cultural and religious sphere of the contemporary world.

Keeping things out of balance

For official institutions – religious and otherwise – stabilty and predictability are centrally important values. Keeping things in a state of balance or equilibrium is the desired state of affairs and the one we naïvely assume to be best suited to growth and progress. In fact, many of these cultural ideals are based on ignorance and fear and a dread of what might happen if we lose the tight grasp that keeps everything in what we perceive to be a secure state of equilibrium.

When we look around at the natural world, we notice that few things are in a state of balance or equilibrium; quite the opposite, in fact. Living creatures are forever changing, growing and developing. Every cell in the human body replicates itself at least once every seven years; what I am today is a totally different person from that of seven years ago. Such are the requirements of growth, change, becoming, progress and development.

Today, we are rediscovering the fundamental instability that is a prequisite for all growth and change, the creative dynamism that offsets the deleterious effects of stagnation and regression. The scientists have named this new wisdom the 'Theory of Chaos', which we will review in Chapter 9. Essentially what the theory highlights is that all change and growth is fuelled by the dynamic interplay of chance, necessity and random processes, which to the human eye seem chaotic and crazy but over time, or at certain imperceptible levels, exhibit harmonies and consistencies that defy human logic. With the aid of chaotic dynamics we can measure many of nature's quirks and irregularities, whether it be unpredictable weather patterns or irregular coastlines. Fractal mathematics which can measure such features highlight the creative potential inherent in the apparently chaotic system. Without the chaos the potential for creative outcomes would be largely diminished, if not absent entirely.

The application to religion and spirituality creates shock waves for those seeking to foster and protect official belief systems. Doubt, uncertainty, syncretism, agnosticism and even atheism are no longer perceived as the arch-enemies of genuine faith, but need to be integrated into the search for an authentic spirituality for our time.

And the guardians of orthodoxy, who consider the maintenance of 'law and order' to be fundamental to dogmatic certitude are challenged to consider the idolatry and ideology which such certainty tends to breed. When everything is clear and certain, Chaos Theory poses disturbing and threatening questions: Whose clarity and certainty are you promulgating – your own or that of the higher authority you claim to be representing? And if you claim to be speaking God's own truth, have you not effectively become Gods in your own right?

Reality can only remain open to the new, to the unexpected, to the future if a sense of imbalance (incompletion) is permitted, respected and encouraged. Only then are we saved from the curse of dogmatism and the many idolatrous Gods in whose names people are oppressed, subdued, tortured, maimed and even sacrificed. Imbalance, with its creative chaos, is not the enemy to be eliminated but the ally that safeguards both the freedom of the spirit and the freedom of the children of God – whose creative interaction are at the basis of all true conversion (cf. Rom. 8:14–17).

Open-ended directionality

Patriarchal consciousness claims that there is only one true way for faith, politics, economics, life. Ultimately, everything must be reduced to this 'one true way'. Variety, diversity, creativity and the use of the imagination are at best suspect; at worst, downright dangerous and subversive.

The monotheistic religions are deemed to be 'more highly developed' because they assert belief in one God rather than many. What we are dealing with here is a humanly devised dualism, a figment of the rational human mind rather than a statement about the meaning of God. Such dualisms – the tendency to divide things into opposing entities – is itself a device invented by our monotheistic culture.

Fortunately, in our time, we are rediscovering the multifarious and multi-dimensional nature of life in what we now understand to be a highly complex planet. The fact that it is complex does not necessarily mean that it is complicated. Complexity is an innate quality of all living systems (organisms, social systems, people, planets) which grow and develop and become more complex in the process of realising their fuller potential.

A growing consciousness is surfacing in today's world that no one field of wisdom or knowledge – not even the religious one – can point us in life's true direction. That direction evolves within the course of evolution itself or, more accurately, co-evolves as each interdependent dimension grows to the realisation of its full potential. For us humans, to attain that fullness of life, we need not only a God to believe in, but we also need the plants of the earth, the fishes of the sea and the many biochemical processes that fertilise creation with beauty and nourishment; destroy any one aspect and human survival becomes precarious, in fact threatened with extinction.

Deterministic ways of understanding life, and the ability to be able to predict various outcomes, underpin the mechanistic sense of directionality that is central to classical science and dogmatic theology. But this rigidly neat and secure world-view is losing credibility at a rapid rate. It no longer resonates with our deep experience (personally or communally) nor with the expanding consciousness of a universe growing in complexity. Gradually, and often reluctantly, the official sciences themselves are forced to ponder the consequences.

There are many features in Ian's story that illustrate this open-ended directionality – yet, it is not a directionless pursuit. The entire enterprise is governed by a conviction of purpose and meaning, and his achievements are clearly goal-oriented, even in the traditional sense of the term. Yet, sealing marriage bonds in a Quaker Centre, celebrating a marriage feast in an open field, choosing to live with his partner in a commune, are not standard and predictable behaviours that meet with common approval. On the contrary, they are perceived as subversive, belittling society's expectations and betraying society's norms (e.g., Ian and Linda did not formalise their marriage according to either state or Church law – they consider such formalities as irrelevant bureaucracy). Yet, many people would laud their originality, creativity and courage for defying and transcending those norms and structures which fail to inspire or animate many people today.

This new sense of open-endedness can lead to anarchy and chaos, but I suggest to no greater an extent than the chaos that we sublimate and repress so effectively in many spheres of contemporary life. The institution of marriage, the nuclear family, the workplace can hide a great deal of loneliness, alienation and destructive violence. But because these are sanctioned institutions of our so-called civilised world, we rarely acknowledge or address the frightening morass which they can foster and maintain.

Open-endedness may be risky and does require a quality of transparency and commitment which seem to be lacking in the liberal culture which is so widespread today. Nonetheless, we must take seriously this new orientation because all indications are that closed systems are on the way out, and open-ended possibilities are going to be the stuff of the future.

I began this chapter with Ian's story which I offer as a parable for the contemporary spiritual search. Ian is an exemplary candidate for this new spiritual vision; few are likely to manage the challenge with such wisdom and integrity. I am not offering his story as a blueprint. In a world of open-ended directionality, there are no blueprints, apart from the Creative Spirit who blows where s(he) wills. And today that Spirit is calling us forth with an outrageously creative freedom, and with surprises that baffle and confuse – particularly those of sturdy faith and solid convictions.

Everything in the spiritual landscape is becoming permeable and porous once more. Despite all our human engineering and the anthropomorphic checks and balances we reinvent time and time again, God's Spirit blows fresh breezes across the barren deserts of sacred traditions and time-honoured institutions. A new day is dawning over the spiritual landscape and new possibilities for spiritual pilgrimage open up on all sides. These new openings and their complex challenges become the subject matter for the remaining chapters of this book.

Narrow boundaries – expanded horizons

Despite frequent comments about secularisation in Western society and a decrease in church membership, there is widespread evidence of a hunger for the spiritual. . . . The interest in spirituality is certainly not confined to church-goers or those commonly identified as religious people.

Philip Sheldrake

I would describe spirituality as the practice of bodily, social, political and personal connectedness so that life comes together in a way that both transcends and includes the bits and pieces that make up our search for wholeness, freedom, relationality, and full human dignity.

Letty M. Russell

Future Christianity is generating itself from the lives of those who have fled to the margins.

Sister Wendy Beckett

A S A CHILD I often roamed the hillsides of southern Ireland. I accompanied my Dad as we rounded up the cattle-herd, cut turf for the winter fires, or hacked gorse to feed the family horse during the winter months. The fragrance of the wild honeysuckle still nourishes my olfactory needs and every time I see wild heather I reconnect with long-lost memories and the innocent thrills of childhood.

Many years on, fortune still provides me with the occasional opportunities to roam those hills once more and savour not merely cherished memories of the past but something of that enduring sacredness echoed in the harshness of mountain rock, the prickly feel of gorse, the smells, the sights, the sounds that beget the reassurance that despite everything else in our troubled world, the mystery within which we live and move is fundamentally benign.

For me, those endearing hillsides are, and always will be, holy ground, a type of oasis where the mystery within and the mystery without communicate in a language and idiom I don't understand,

and possibly never will; nor does it in any way perturb me that I don't fully comprehend. One stretch of hillside has changed significantly in recent years with the erection of a grotto to Our Lady of Lourdes, a landmark now known throughout Ireland for the sensationalism of a 'moving statue'.

With the discovery of the 'moving statue' crowds began to flock to the grotto; rosaries were said, novenas were prayed; people kept silence and at times chattered ceaselessly. Some claimed to have been healed and to be the recipients of miraculous cures. Whatever about the marvel of the 'moving statue', it certainly got people praying and recreated a fresh sense of God in people's lives – at least, that's what some people felt and assiduously communicated that message in both public and private media.

Eventually the nine-days wonder began to wane; the crowds dwindled to the odd passer-by, so once again the grotto could enjoy its silent harmony with the natural hillside. The occasional tourist or passer-by will stop and pray, bless themselves with water from the stream, drop a donation in the box and move on. Whether it is duty fulfilled or intercession enacted, the visit to the grotto has answered a need. For the moment, at least, the spiritual task is complete.

In just a few years the grotto became a spiritual or religious focus to an extent which the hillside itself had never assumed; yet the sacred story of that hillside outlives the grotto by millennia and embodies a divine creativity that can never be condensed into any one spiritual focus, object or otherwise. Although the grotto has a unique beauty, it is only a dim reflection of the spiritual energy and co-creativity embodied in the hillside itself. The statues are carved by human hand and measured to human perception and need; the structure, though sensitively designed, is also a human workpiece. The hillside is the work of another designer, more elegant and creative than anything we humans can ever hope to emulate.

So why don't we pray to the hillside? Why don't we bless ourselves with its flowing streams and luscious growth? Why don't we donate to its ongoing development just as it contributes unceasingly to the joy and sense of wonder it bestowed on me as a child – and still does? What is it that makes the grotto sacred in a way that the hillside is not? Or is that even the appropriate question!

Echoes that muzzle the mystery

There are many people eager to rush in and offer answers to my questions. I hear echoes arising from my inherited past, some from the super-ego within and many from the orthodox world without. Although all are well intended, the patronising overtones are all too audible. However, let's try to hear the concerns – and perhaps, the challenges – that are inherent in these observations.

1. *But the hillside is impersonal – there is no guarantee that this experience will lead you to a personal relationship with Jesus Christ.*
In statements like this, what do we mean by 'person' and 'personal'? Presumably, we are speaking out of our experience of what it means to be a human being, and out of those relationships and friendships that enable us to define what we mean by the 'personal'. And in applying the word 'relationship' to Jesus Christ might we not be projecting onto the divine experiences that effectively belong to the human realm? I am not suggesting that we refrain from using such terms in a religious context; I am inviting a deeper reflection and dialogue on why we choose to use such images and ideas.

Our Christian inheritance (and indeed the spiritual traditions of many of the great religions) bequeaths to us a set of images and understandings very much focused on human personhood as we have understood and enculturated it throughout the ages. One such time-honoured, but also time-constricted, caricature is that with which we portray the Jesus of Christianity: male, white, bearded and adorned in Romanesque dress. Quite understandably, that image is becoming problematic for many people today; in fact, if that were not the case, we would be dealing with some dangerous ideologies.

The 'personal relationship with Jesus' is hailed by many spiritual guides as the ultimate criterion of a mature spirituality. I, too, have had times when I felt God to be very close and reassuring; in fact, I frequently experience such feelings when I roam my favourite hillsides, walk along the seashore, meander in the open countryside on a moonlit night, or sit quietly in a chapel. Yet, I hesitate to use a human analogy to explain that experience because it feels as though something greater and more profound is at work.

I then find myself challenged to pose these questions: To what extent is our anthropocentric compulsiveness – 'man is the measure of all things' – the dominant underlying motivation of the focus on the personal relationship with Jesus? Are we not in danger of reducing God-in-Jesus to our image and likeness? And, insofar as the relationship tends to be described in patriarchal terms (even in the case of the loving father) is there not a subtle spiritualism at work, seeking to elicit subservience and compliance that may be quite alien to the freedom of the children of God?

Admittedly, the closest comparison we humans can find to describe those loving and relational feelings that may surface in prayer, or in times of spiritual uplift, is that of our human relationships, or rather, the ideals we seek to explore and experience within those interactions. Lofty though such experiences may be at times, they remain human, couched in the limited concepts and descriptions of human intelligence which in turn is affected and coloured by social and cultural norms and expectations.

The fact that my hillside dialogue with the divine cannot be easily explained or comprehended in human terms may be precisely its greatest authentication. Might it not also be the more generalised field of spiritual experience within which all credal-based responses need to be discerned? In much of the literature, the journey from the particular (religion) to the general (spiritual landscape) is considered to be normative for the spiritual journey. Is this the manageable, linear and rational package that suited the specific consciousness of a previous age? The emerging consciousness of our time suggests the very opposite: from the general to the particular; my limited familiarity with the great mystics indicates that they, too, adopt this latter orientation.

2. *It sounds a bit pagan to me – worshipping the elements like people did in primitive times.*
Beneath this statement one hears echoes of phobias, projections and often a substantial measure of moral self-righteousness. At the conscious level, statements like this are intended to convey certitude and clarity of faith, but subconsciously they may be motivated by a great deal of ignorance, fear and irrational ideology.

What is particularly disturbing is the apparent ease with which we often label people, because we don't like what they are saying or doing. Commonly-used labels of our culture include: conservative, radical, socialist, agnostic, heretic, schizophrenic, homosexual, evangelical. Unknowingly, our patriarchal culture often uses labels to put people in their place. Frequently, people themselves become so co-opted into the prevailing system that they themselves adopt the labels in an attempt to find identity in a confusing world.

'Pagan' is a label liberally used in Christian discourse. It denotes not merely opposition to formal religion, but also the devotion of one's time and energy to worshipping 'objects' perceived to be replacements for the real God. The word embodies a certitude of truth whereby those who deviate are judged as condemned and damned for eternity. It mirrors the closed ideology of Christendom rather than the open, spiritual search that begets many so-called pagan cultures.

The statement becomes even more convoluted when it alleges that ancient worship of sun, moon, stars, etc. was primitive. This is a classical patriarchal projection: what we (men in particular) who belong to the era of civilisation (approximately, the past 5,000 years) consider to be civilised, we declare to be superior to all that went before it. True worship of God is only possible in a civilised culture – and in the eyes of patriarchy that has to be monotheistic in nature. It should be fairly obvious who is playing God here!

The ability and freedom to perceive our ancient past in a more favourable light is one of the supreme spiritual challenges of our time. As indicated elsewhere in this book, we are not about a contemporary fad of exonerating the past, but stretching the horizons of our self-understanding as a human-planetary species. More about that in subsequent chapters.

3. *That's the danger with all these 'new age' people – they don't know what they're praying to or worshipping.*
If you ever want to test the intolerance of those who claim to be ardently committed to the Christian gospel, simply use the words 'new age' and you are likely to experience one of the quickest personality changes you have ever witnessed! We are dealing with a label that elicits very deep feelings. Some of the strongest reactions come from those who – for a range of complex reasons – perceive the 'new age' movement as potentially threatening to mainstream Christianity in a way that few other movements are.

Again, the subconscious undergirding needs special attention, normally not offered, nor allowed, by those who consider themselves to be the official guardians of truth and holiness. There is a prevalent perception that movements such as 'new age' lure people – especially the young – away from the church and from the formal practice of the faith; I am not aware of any evidence to substantiate this claim. The 'new age' movement seems more attractive to those who have not had any explicit faith tradition, and are seeking new forms of spiritual fellowship (see the informative work of Saliba, 1995).

As a movement, we tend to judge the 'new age' by its exaggerated overt practices: opting out of the mainstream culture; tribal tendencies and behaviours; liberal modes of intimate and sexual relations; a tendency to dabble in drugs, etc. The more we focus on the externals, the greater the risk that we will miss the covert meaning which, I suggest, belongs to the genre of spiritual and cultural evolution. The 'new age', as various researchers point out, has many millennial characteristics, typifying the dynamics that tend to accompany the 'end of an age' epoch. If that perception is even broadly correct, then 'new age' followers are more likely to be 'acting out' subconsciously what millions across the world are experiencing, rather than consciously perpetuating a philosophy of their own making.

The dominant polarity in the 'new age' consciousness tends to manifest in a tension between:

1. those who are so wearied and disillusioned with the old reality – and its inevitable demise – that they see no point in continuing to promote its growth, or alternatively want to throw it overboard completely and
2. those who want to place all their resourcefulness at the service of the new, perceived to be in radical discontinuity with the old.

What at first may seem a rather extreme set of views, are, in fact, profoundly biblical in both content and vision. We have all the ingredients of a paschal journey, except in this case applied to a major cultural transition rather than to a human being. Many contemporary theorists acknowledge that our world today is undergoing breakdown and disintegration, a cultural Calvary that defies rational explanation (e.g., Burrows, Mayne & Newbury, 1991; Drucker, 1989; Sahtouris, 1989; Zohar, 1993). Many of those same theorists allude to a paradigm shift, a cultural, global Resurrection, so radically new that it requires a profound change of mind and heart to comprehend its meaning. As a counter-cultural movement of our time, the 'new age' seems to be evoking an eminently timely spiritual revolution, one that could rock the foundations of Christendom, but not the central challenge of Christianity.

4. *If we all choose to follow this creation-centred spirituality, what will happen to the church and the sacraments?*
Once again, there are resounding echoes of fear – of losing what we have so long cherished, of betraying our sacred traditions, of rocking the religious edifices to a degree that might reap havoc. If we could face that fear and move deeper to a more reflective space, we could both ask and answer the question: What is the source of the fear in the first place? In fact, it comes from a deep personal and planetary need for sacred space, for ritual, sacrament and church as living communion.

Contemporary Christian theology affirms unambiguously that the task of the church is to be and to build community; but for the vast majority of 'practising' Christians, this theory does not translate into practical action. The church is considered to be a moralistic, clericalised organisation that dictates moral guidelines and provides sacramental experience, employing symbols and rituals, many of which have outlived their symbolic usefulness.

As a prophetic community that acts for the liberation of the poor, the church has a spiritual and political appeal for some marginalised underclasses of the southern hemisphere, especially in Latin America. It is difficult to gauge how widely and deeply shared this conviction is, since there are strong indications that people tend to abandon the church as their economic and social status improves.

That the church is the Body of Christ, the living community in which the Resurrected One is primarily embodied in the power of word and sacrament, is a theological and spiritual conviction shared by few apart from an intellectual elite. Consequently, those who echo the fear that commitment to church and sacrament is shallow and could be even further eroded are probably justified in holding that fear. However, it is what fuels the fear, rather than the fear itself that needs deeper discernment.

One central dilemma is a universal tendency to build religious commitment on very shaky spiritual foundations. There exists a widespread conviction that religion precedes spirituality, that spiritual growth is impossible apart from religious adherence, and for Christians this means that there is no authentic spirituality apart from faith in Jesus Christ as the revelation of the one true God.

Here we touch on a perennial issue as we search for a more integrated spirituality. The spiritual feelings that arise in my heart as I walk the 'sacred' hillsides of Ireland will arise in my heart whether I have a religious upbringing or not; the precondition for that experience is not formation in a specific religious system but an openness to the creative Spirit of wisdom and love who inhabits the whole of creation and dwells in my inner being, informing my every instinct and my desire for meaning.

My formal faith tradition will enable me to name my experience, to couch it in words and concepts which will assist in deepening the experience and will enable me to engage with others in shared spiritual discourse, the basis for any authentic participation in the community of the church. The temptation here is that the ability to name can also become the occasion to label, to box things into categories that belong to the linear and literalist mind-set, to establish immutable dogmas.

The hillside spiritual awakening can be a purifying element in a movement that otherwise can become distorted and even convoluted. Nature helps to bring us back to basics, vividly illustrated in Ian's story (Chapter 1); it never ceases to remind us that the God who seeks us out is the One that is more vast, yet more intimate, than that enculturated in any system or dogma, ecclesiastical or otherwise.

Our spiritual malnutrition

Over the centuries we have amassed an enormous repertoire of spiritual expertise ranging from schools of spirituality with their respective gurus and disciples; scholars who try to plumb the depths of both soul and spirit; techniques and methods that claim to produce fulfilment and liberation. Yet, few would deny that there is something fundamentally amiss in our spiritual tradition; in fact, many feel a kind of suffocation of spiritual overload. It feels as if something essential has been ignored or bypassed in the accumulation of spiritual baggage, down through the ages.

My favourite hillside has its special places, little oases, that provide a more hallowed space in which I can allow more dangerous and delicate questions to unravel. Connecting into my own spiritual journey, I find the following hungers arise quite frequently these days:

1. *I hunger for a spiritual nourishment that involves something more than the Catholic Church is offering me.*

Here I share from my own denominational base, but in doing so, I wish to be inclusive of all those who still look to their respective churches for spiritual nourishment, and having looked frequently, come away still starving and disillusioned. I identify in particular with the vast numbers of people who, implicitly or explicitly, feel that church should be much more overtly and consciously fostering the lay dimension of its identity and ministry.

Currently, the Catholic Church universally consists of 1.1 billion members, 99 per cent of whom are lay people of non-clerical status. Yet, anywhere and everywhere I turn, I find that church is both defined and activated primarily according to the rules and expectations of its governing clerical body. Ultimately, whether in the North, South or Far East, it is clericalism that runs and controls the Catholic Church. Innate to such clericalism is a patriarchal, subconscious driving force which is much more about power in the name of religion, rather than about service in the name of spirituality.

As a lay person, I feel I don't belong any more in the closed world of clerical domination; I am weary of power games, ritualism, moralism and all the empty rhetoric. I am more interested in egalitarianism, vulnerability, prophetic contestation, engaging with the God of the flesh, the God of passion, the God of real personal, interpersonal, and earthly incarnation.

2. *I hunger for a spiritual nourishment that transcends the polemics of religious imperialism.*

In the popular version of our Christian faith, there prevails a type of theological imperialism which I feel I have often colluded with in the past and which I now perceive to be arrogant and oppressive. I refer to the Christian claim (to which Judaism and Islam also subscribe) that our religion contains the fullness of revelation, in the light of which all other religions are deemed to be somehow inferior. What perturbs me particularly are the ideological and political implications of this stance, and the collusions Christians entertain in order to foster – especially in the two-thirds world – our imperialistic, oppressive belief-system. On the one hand, we preach gospel liberation, yet we lure people into subjugation in the name of a divine claim which in reality is a convoluted, anthropocentric control mechanism, just one of the several at which our patriarchal culture is quite adept.

It seems to me that Christians have deviated quite seriously from the central message of the Christian gospel: the New Reign of God (Kingdom) promised to all, a radically new egalitarian community characterised by justice, love, peace and liberation. In trying to enculturate this message over the centuries, we have extrapolated Christ from the Kingdom vision and made him the subject of a personality cult which, when theologically translated, becomes the 'Head of the Church'.

Jesus did not preach himself; he told stories about the Basileia (Greek word for Kingdom) of love and liberation, and invited his followers to be salt of the earth and light for the world, inspired by that same spiritual vision. We need to transcend the narrow focus on the individual hero whom we have made so heavenly that we frequently betray the incarnational engagement which seems to have been central to Jesus' own life and for which people are hungering today.

3. *In seeking fresh spiritual pastures, I entered the world of multi-faith dialogue, but that, too, leaves me feeling undernourished.*
Multi-faith dialogue is very much a development of the latter half of the twentieth century, matching the expanding and more inclusive sense with which we seek to address many global issues of our time. Initiated, and still maintained, largely by Christians (see Tracy, 1994; Hick, 1995; Knitter, 1995), it seeks to promote dialogue and mutual interaction between adherents of the various creeds while seeking to respect the unique beliefs and customs of each religious system. In the co-operative exchange of feelings and views, many people experience a growing awareness of the one God who unites us all, irrespective of our particular religious allegiance.

For spiritual seekers of our time, the multi-faith dialogue feels like 'too little, too late'. It continues to couch spirituality in the categories and limited vision of formal religion. And in its desperate attempt to be all-inclusive, it evades or bypasses questions of allegiance and difference which are fundamentally sectarian, prejudiced, oppressive, exclusive (e.g., of women) and, at times, verging on the idolatrous. Despite the good will, the spiritual vision underpinning multi-faith dialogue continues to be removed from, and alien to, the real world in which the majority of human beings struggle for hope and meaning in their daily lives.

4. *I hunger for a spirituality at the heart of creation, and increasingly, this feels incompatible with adherence to formal religion.*
The mountain air is clear and fresh, like the eternal breath of the Spirit of life. Often I sit at the rock face and let my eyes linger on the surrounding landscape. One gets an intuitive sense that these rocks have been around for a long time; their hardness and solidity convey a feeling of an enduring reality.

There is an awakening sense that I, too, have been around for a long time. My species has walked this earth for an estimated 4.4 million years; as creatures who stand upright, for 2 million years. It is over 600,000 years since we invented fire, a highly significant moment in our awakening spiritual consciousness. Anthropologists and archaeologists inform us that we have exhibited distinctly spiritual behaviour and values for at least 70,000 years. Perhaps, most enthralling of all, is the highly artistic and creative spiritual ferment focused around the Great Earth Mother Goddess, that informed our spiritual awareness as a universal species for an estimated 35,000 years (from c. 40000–5000 BCE).

These are the thoughts that go through my mind as I sit at the rock face, and I ask myself: How is it that our theology and spirituality never refers to these realities? Why does our supreme religious wisdom choose to ignore the elegant divine–human co-creativity across the expansive wonder and beauty of creation? Why do most books on spirituality allude only to the Christian experience as if God did not even exist prior to Christian times? Is it possible that our anthropocentric needs have become so self-absorbing that we are in danger of suffocating ourselves in a religious enclave devoid of mystery, wonder and breadth?

Increasingly, I find myself in sympathy with the spiritual seekers who claim that formal religion, with its trappings and power games, is proving to be a major obstacle to spiritual growth and development. Religion sets limitations, and lures the seeker into dealing with issues which seem to belong to the perpetuation of the system rather than the growth of the person. The system in turn, instead of empowering the person to engage with the world in a transformative way, inhibits, and often directly militates against, the task of transformative justice. The anti-world polemic still dominates the formal religions.

Which Christian metaphor: boundary or horizon ?

These reflections are often perceived with a mixture of sadness and fear. Sadness, that a believing Christian like myself could deviate so far from what is perceived to be the true faith. Fear, that the waver-ing or unconverted might find these views attractive and thus veer even further away from the way of orthodoxy. I would like to record my gratitude – to God and to people – for the Christian faith I have inherited, a faith that has nourished and sustained me – and still does – through the diverse experiences of life. For me, that faith remains, and I guess always will be, foundational: it is the starting point from which everything else unfolds.

My early upbringing emphasised not so much the uniqueness of Christianity as its exclusiveness: 'Outside the church there's no sal-vation.' I was almost twenty years of age when I met my first Protestant; my prejudice, sectarianism and bigotry was so deeply rooted that I terminated our dialogue after the initial greeting. Were it not for the fact that life produced a few 'divine surprises' that jolted me out of my closed world-view, e.g. the invitation to share in an ecumenical Eucharist on my first trip to Taizé, or a train con-versation with a British soldier who four days later was shot dead by my fellow-countrymen, I may well have remained locked in my ideological security. My first counselling session with a Muslim cou-ple proved to be another memorable moment of spiritual liberation.

As I continue to engage with the spiritual agendas of our time – and my perception is that there is a widespread and profound spir-itual hunger in today's world – I encounter two dominant Christian approaches. The first, and most prevalent, continues to be a closed, stultifying model often presented with a veneer of modernity and inclusiveness. Theologically, it goes something like this: Jesus Christ, as Messiah, embodies the fullness of God's revelation for humanity. Jesus is the measure and completion of all things, includ-ing the religious and spiritual aspirations of all time. Spiritual growth demands total submission to Jesus so that we can become totally like him in this life and live with him for ever after death.

This is called the boundary model, with its patriarchal, male, white Saviour firmly ensconced like a king on a royal throne (the dominant metaphor for much of the Christian era), and in whose name everything is prescribed and validated. Boundaries are set: theological, ethical, spiritual, ritual, within which orthodoxy prevails and outside of which one is considered to be unfaithful on a spectrum stretching from the 'dubious' to 'outright heresy'. The great danger I see here is that in setting boundaries around the religious system, we also hem in the living Spirit and, theologically, we pursue questions which have more to do with our needs than an understanding of God's life in us or for us, e.g. the ongoing debate about the historical Jesus. Evangelical groups and movements adhere to the boundary model in a particularly vitriolic way, shielding the spiritually malnourished and petrified with an idolatrous God image, largely designed on the childish fears of insecure human beings.

The American theologian Marc C. Taylor offers the following description of theology (or what he calls 'a/theology'): 'A permeable membrane that forms a border where fixed boundaries disintegrate' (Taylor, 1984, p. 12). The boundary model of traditional and mainstream Christianity has outlived its usefulness, but more seriously, as writers like Taylor intimate, this model may be fundamentally alien to the vision and mission of our Christian faith.

As an alternative to the boundary, I propose the horizon model, one which embodies in a more integrated way the aspirations of many spiritual seekers of our time. We are dealing with an open system, focusing on Christ the primordial embodiment of God's New Reign in creation which continues to grow and develop until the end of time. Our starting point here is what the gospels call the New Reign of God (for the sake of inclusiveness, I tend to use the Greek, Basileia), the trans-cultural faith community for which Jesus is the first and exemplary disciple. This is, above all else, a community of mission, catapulting its members into the heart of creation, where all creatures (and not just humans) co-create with God until the Kingdom comes in its fullness.

For Christians, the church is called to be the exemplary community that celebrates both the present reality and future challenge of the Basileia, a task which the church today seems unable to assume or facilitate. Consequently, spiritual seekers of our time don't look to the church for enlightenment or guidance; many who do, become even more confused and disillusioned. Today, the spiritual ferment outside the church, at the cutting edge of the Basileia horizon, is what touches the heart and fires the imagination of the spiritual seeker, and not the staid ritualism and empty rhetoric of an outdated and increasingly irrelevant institution.

Retrieving the primacy of the spiritual

Our reflections raise even more profound questions for contemporary spirituality, recurring questions posed by many of the great mystics down through the ages. The Jesus who inaugurated the vision of the Basileia, and continues to foster it as Risen Cosmic Saviour, is about something larger, more expansive and more inclusive than the church, but also about something more profound than formal religion. We tend to assume that Jesus came to establish a new religion, and we went ahead and invented a religious system in his name, a cultural strategy that may have been necessary to establish Christianity as a religious and moral force, but the price we paid was a fundamental betrayal of what gives heart and soul to the Christian faith in the first place, namely the Basileia.

There is a growing realisation among contemporary theologians that the Basileia cannot be reduced to any cultural system, religious or otherwise (a topic I explore at length in Chapter 9). We are dealing with something that is essentially global, egalitarian and inclusive of all peoples and cultures. The engagement with the Kingdom is not just about the confined world of formal religion (the boundary model), but about the evolutionary horizons that relate to the fullness of life, personal, interpersonal, planetary and cosmic.

Could it be, therefore, as Sheehan (1986) suggests, that Jesus was not just about the transformation of religion, but rather about the end of religion? In evolutionary and cosmological terms, could it be that religion is merely a temporary reality that may well have achieved its purpose, and perhaps is now outliving its usefulness? The experience of many contemporary spiritual seekers – outlined in Chapter 1 – suggests that large numbers of people are outgrowing the need for formal religion. They seek spirituality, but not religion. The retrieval of spirituality as the primary dynamic of human, spiritual growth may be the supreme challenge facing humanity in the next millennium. It is an exciting, but daunting, prospect.

Before we explore the significance of this new challenge, we review the story of spirituality as it unfolds in the light of contemporary research. The story will beget its own meaning, and point to the many issues and engagements which recur down through the ages as the human spirit continues to articulate the divine restlessness which underpins and motivates all our spiritual aspirations.

— 3 —

Encountering the spirit world

In the infinite variety and complexity of the universe it is so that upon the earth energy has become living matter and matter has become self-reflective and feels itself.

Julie Hopkins

The natural world is the maternal source of our being . . . (it) is the larger sacred community to which we belong. To be alienated from this community is to become destitute in all that makes us human.

Thomas Berry

OUR WORLD TODAY is engulfed in a kind of spiritual schizophrenia, based on a dualistic set of perceptions whereby we divide reality into the opposing categories of God versus man(kind), spirit versus matter, the sacred versus the secular. This in fact, is a deconstruction of our God-given reality, a way of thinking and behaving that undermines the spiritual and cultural wholeness of life. And there is a great deal of evidence to suggest that religion itself contributes significantly to this dilemma.

We make the assumption that spirituality is concomitant with civilisation which we usually date back to about 3000 BCE, with the rise of the first cities among the Sumerian people of Mesopotamia. Consequently, spirituality, as popularly conceived, is closely linked to the evolution of formal religions over the past 5,000 years. Adherence to one or other religion is considered a prerequisite for spiritual growth and maturation – or at least, this was the case until very recent times. And each religion has developed its own spiritual vision, quite independent of the others and at times fiercely opposed to every other spiritual tradition. Submission in thought and action to a God-like figure, according to a specific set of prescriptions or guidelines, is considered to be essential to an authentic spiritual journey. And the final destination is the achievement of salvation, nirvana, enlightenment in a place or realm beyond and outside this imperfect, spiritually deficient world.

Sacred and profane space

Religious anthropologists, of whom Joachim Wach, Ninian Smart, B. Malinowski, Joseph Campbell and Mircea Eliade are leading authorities, do not search for spirituality in the world of formal religious belief. Instead they seek to explore a more ancient tradition, remnants of which they believe are still preserved in tribal rituals and customs of recent centuries and decades (cf. Barnes, 1984; Schmidt, 1980). Central to such research is the concept of a sacred space over against that of profane space, a topic frequently recurring in the works of Mircea Eliade (1961, 1978), probably the greatest religious anthropologist of recent times. According to Eliade (1961, p. 20), there are parts of space that are qualitatively different as indicated in God's command to Moses: 'Do not come near; put off your shoes from your feet, for the place on which you are standing is holy ground' (Exod. 3:5).

There is, then, a sacred space, and hence a strong, significant space; there are other spaces that are not sacred and so are without structure or consistency, amorphous. Nor is this all. For religious man, this spatial non-homogeneity finds expression in the experience of an opposition between space that is sacred – the only real and real-ly existing space – and all other space, the formless expanse surrounding it.

For Eliade, the sacred space is the indispensible locus in which those spiritually transformative experiences, fundamental to human meaning, are activated. It is the wellspring of creativity and renewal that activates and potentiates order and harmony, especially in the encounter with chaos and destruction. It is also a safeguard against the false enthusiasm that tends to rush in 'where angels dare not tread'. In Eliade's view, such an unprepared encounter with the spiritual world could have many deleterious consequences, including psychic and spiritual damage to the human personality.

Initiation rites, therefore, are of immense significance for an appropriate engagement with the spiritual journey. Many such rituals, even to this day, imply a *regressus ad uterum* (return to the womb), symbolised for example in the immersion in water, as performed in Christian baptism. Re-entering the womb, being re-born into one's true identity, is also considered to have cosmological significance: the neophyte also belongs to the womb of Mother Earth and requires her nurturing sustenance to live meaningfully in the world. Personal and planetary integration are considered to occur simultaneously in Rites of Passage related to initiation.

The concept of sacred space highlights the need for a special mode of being, and sometimes a hallowed place (e.g. church, temple or gurdwara) if we are to nourish our spiritual hunger, especially in the case of public worship. However, the concept also carries overtones of patriarchal influence that need to be addressed. The sacred and secular are set in dualistic opposition, with the sacred always considered the more real and authentic; this quickly develops into a dualistic anthropology whereby the person outside the sacred space remains fundamentally unspiritual, a conviction that Eliade clearly rejects in his claim that the sacred is an element in the structure of consciousness, not a stage in the history of consciousness. The sacred space therefore provides a nurturing ambience wherein spirituality grows and flourishes, rather than a precondition for its emergence in the first place.

These reflections pose a number of challenges:

1. Spirituality is an innate quality of human life and existence. It is something we are born with, something essentially dynamic that forever seeks articulation and expression in human living.
2. Spirituality is one of life's great gifts to us, and we have been entrusted with its care and development.
3. Spirituality is essentially a co-creative gift; we are partially, but not wholly, reponsible for its development. As in the exchange of all gifts, there is the giver and the receiver, but unlike the normal process, the gift in this case is forever being offered and received, in large or small measure.
4. The gift we refer to is life in all those dimensions that can be explored and developed throughout an entire lifetime, lived creatively and meaningfully in mutual relation with planet Earth and the cosmos. A meaningful spiritual life is inconceivable without a meaningful planetary and cosmic existence.
5. There are both conscious and subconscious factors involved in spiritual growth. Because spirituality is innate to the human personality, we are always living out of a spiritual will-to-meaning,

but it might not always be appropriately expressed. For example, participation in a wedding banquet is a highly spiritual activity, with a great range of ritual and symbolic interaction that touch into the core of human relatedness (and consequently to the core of human meaning), but in today's Western world, the powerful spiritual energies at work are largely unacknowledged and very poorly integrated.

6. Spiritual energy is at least as powerful as, and probably more powerful than, our strongest instinctual drives and desires. Consequently, a thwarted spiritual drive, or one not appropriated consciously, will often seek expression in dangerous, destructive, or pathological behaviours. A great deal of youth culture, especially drug-related, is fuelled by a misguided spiritual hunger; so is a great deal of economic or sexual prowess in the adult population. I suggest it is more accurate to view these developments as unintegrated spiritual overload rather than an absence of a spiritual sense. Spirituality cannot be absent in a human life, but it can be misguided and misplaced to a degree that ensues in horrendous destruction – personally, socially and culturally.

The notion of 'sacred space' is better understood today as a realm of inner experience, innate to every human being, that requires our conscious and informed attention if it is to come to full flowering. The realm of spiritual experience is not a static one; like all God's gifts its nature is to grow, unfold and become. Almost in spite of ourselves, that primordial divinised energy will seek outlet and expression; whether such expression is benign or destructive largely depends on our understanding and internalisation of our spiritual giftedness.

The development of our spirituality requires not one, but several 'sacred' spaces. In early childhood, it needs a loving and trusting environment; we are all familiar with the after-effects of early childhood trauma which truly can reach satanic proportions. In adolescence, it requires an environment of respect and support to question, doubt, rebel and indulge the agnostic for a while; in early adulthood, it requires an enlightened, adult response, and not the naïve answers that are offered to placate young children, or seek to keep the rebellious adolescent within the ranks of the believing community.

At many other stages through the journey of life, our spiritual hunger is best nourished through appropriate rituals and communal celebrations that affirm us in our achievements and sustain us in our struggles. In all these examples, there is the tension between the sacred space that nourishes solitude and that which provides for social and interpersonal interaction. Finally, there is the more recent awareness, that different personality types may also require distinctive spiritual spaces to bring to fuller realisation their spiritual potential.

Alongside the inner dimension of sacred space is an important outer one. There is a growing realisation in the spiritual consciousness of our time that all space is sacred and that the inner realm remains largely vacuous if we remain disenchanted with the 'god' we encounter in our daily, earthly lives. It is this latter dimension – the planetary and cosmic context – that needs our primary attention, since it has been largely subverted and seriously undermined throughout the epoch of formal religion, and for long before that. It is this global understanding of the sacred space that will concern us primarily in this and subsequent chapters.

Shedding the dualistic cosmology

The cosmology underpinning the major world religions was, and continues to be, essentially mechanistic and functional. It is substantially a dualistic world-view driven and maintained by an insatiable desire to divide and conquer. For all the religions, the ultimate goal is that of happiness and fulfilment in the heavenly realm of completion and perfection. In all cases this world of ultimate fulfilment is considered to be somewhere 'beyond', and will eventually absorb the world we know and experience in our daily lives.

In contradistinction to the 'other world' (heaven, hell, purgatory), we use the phrase 'this world' to denote the here-and-now reality of our daily lives. In the spiritual literature, the term 'this world' tends to have a rather negative connotation, depicting the physical creation (which could be either planet Earth or the entire cosmos) as a purely physical place, transitory in nature and inhabited by evil forces and influences. It seems to resemble that dimension of creation which classical science depicts as dead inert matter, inhabited by humans whose exploitation and selfishness seem to be intermeshed with the precariousness of the world itself.

Whatever the precise explanation, we end up with a classical dualism: the next world, home to all those humans who have evolved into the fullness of spirit, denoting all that is complete and perfect; and this world, signifying the realm of incompleteness, transitoriness and sin, territory that is alien to the spiritual life. Traditionally the task of spirituality, exercised through the ministry of the church, was to provide people with the wherewithal to get from this world to the next; only in the next life could salvation be guaranteed.

Contemporary spirituality (and theology) issues an unambiguous invitation to let go of the old, dualistic cosmology. It has served its time and purpose. It no longer speaks meaningfully to our contemporary experience. It no longer makes sense, and from a cosmological point of view, never did. The desire to fragment the world into dualistic categories is a human construct, not a cosmological nor a divine fact. It is an anthropomorphic imposition that represents the human will to power but not the divine will to co-create. The dualistic cosmology is fundamentally a false representation of what reality is about. It grossly distorts and exploits the notion of sacred space.

What this book calls 'The New Cosmology' (explored at length in Chapter 5) is not entirely new. Mystics have been in touch with it for millennia. Our prehistoric ancestors were aware of it, obviously within a different spiritual and intellectual ambience from ours. It underpins a great deal of African, Asian and South American culture, grossly overshadowed by the Christian imperialism of the northern hemisphere.

Our spiritualised universe

With the decline of Christian imperialism, we witness a revival in creation-based spirituality, a rediscovery of the sacred within the created order itself. This often involves a sense of interconnectedness with other life-forms and with the cosmos at large, which in turn ensues in a growing appreciation of the fundamental unity of everything within creation. Not surprisingly, therefore, the United Nations now invites people all over the world to celebrate One World Week on an annual basis, just a small reminder that our world is one, not a set of dualistic opposites. The sacred 'places' previously described as the next world we now understand to be realms of being within the one world. Heaven, hell, purgatory, are all states of being within the one world! Our ultimate fulfilment is not to be sought in escaping to a life beyond, but in a fuller engagement within the landscape of the cosmos itself.

Even research into the physical sciences is evoking a distinctive spiritual awakening among scientists and others whose professional task often requires rigorous, non-religious allegiance. Scan through any of the books on the 'new physics' and one notices a strong spiritual flavour (e.g. Davies, 1992; Ferguson, 1994; Matthews, 1992). Evolutionary studies increasingly point us toward a world of enormous elegance, complexity and beauty, far beyond anything the human mind has ever dreamt of (a topic I have explored at length in Ó Murchú, 1997). And for 98 per cent of that time the evolutionary process unfolded without any assistance from us. From within its own creative potential the cosmos produced the stars, the galaxies, the sun, the moon, the planets, the many creatures who inhabit the Earth (and perhaps, unknown to us, creatures who inhabit other planets), and finally us, humans.

It is no longer appropriate to think of the ultimate purpose of the evolutionary process as designed to produce intelligent creatures like us – the so-called Anthropic-Cosmological principle.[4] From an evolutionary point of view there is nothing to suggest that we are the ultimate species; quite the contrary, everything points to the fact that creatures more developed than ourselves will evolve in due course. One of the major shifts in consciousness required for our time is that we belong to the evolutionary co-creative process, and it is in rediscovering our mutual interdependence with the cosmos, and particularly with planet Earth, that we will begin to reclaim our spiritual identity. This will require a painful letting-go of our anthropocentric will-to-power that one time brainwashed us into thinking that we were the masters of creation (Gen. 1:26–28) and still deludes us into believing that we are essential to the whole evolutionary process.

We need to remind ourselves frequently that the divinely animated course of evolution wove its own elegant tapestry without any human assistance long before we humans ever emerged from within that same creative process. Evolution alone, despite all its unanswered – and perhaps, unanswerable – questions, is overladen with meaning (better described as a sense of direction rather than a sense of purpose). Deep within the creative process there is an activation of spirit power, which I believe is an inescapable fact to the eyes of the searching heart.

Even in the event of a global catastrophe, such as nuclear annihilation, creation will continue to evolve without us humans. Our uniqueness in evolutionary terms is in our capacity to co-create within the creative process of evolution itself and to serve that process in its becoming conscious of itself. This may well be the most revolutionary tenet of a renewed spirituality for our time.

From a spiritual perspective, we also need to heed current research on the nature of empty space in the universe (cf. Davidson, 1989; Laszlo, 1993). The empty space is often identified with the ether, a comparison Albert Einstein and others quickly dismissed. Nevertheless, the notion has prevailed and it is now considered a core dimension of the energy that enlivens everything in our world. Some 90 per cent of the space in the universe is emptiness, in the sense that it is not occupied by tangible, physical reality. What we now realise is that that emptiness is in fact a fullness, a reservoir of pure energy that continuously potentiates, begets and holds the entire universal creative process in being. Without the creative vacuum, everything would dissolve into nothingness. Emptiness is the precondition for the fullness of life in the universe, a wisdom long known and cherished in the great religions of the East, particularly in Buddhism.

The vacuum may be described as a spiritual energy, the nearest scientific description for which might be the Jungian notion of the Collective Unconscious. For Jung the Collective Unconscious is like a mass envelope of creative, divinely-endowed energy surrounding the entire cosmos. Jung developed the notion mainly in terms of human consciousness which at all times and circumstances is influenced by the power of the Collective Unconscious. Many scholars – scientists and psychologists – note the close connection with that of the creative vacuum.

A world inhabited by spirit

These reflections provide a useful backdrop to the material of this chapter on the notion of the spirit world. There are many esoteric sciences that dabble in issues related to the spirit world ranging from astrology, mediumship, witchcraft, to the invocation of spirit-guides, etc. Across the ages, humans tried to connect and engage with other life-forms in the 'higher' realms. It is an age-old pursuit, but with immense following in today's world, and often commanding more fascination and allegiance than the wisdom of official religious or spiritual practices. Such fascination tends to be judgmentally and naïvely dismissed as 'an interest in the occult', thereby undermining the possibility of a more comprehensive analysis that might prove quite enlightening in our attempts to understand the spiritual hunger of our time.

It is this climate of suspicion and superficial judgment that inhibits a more comprehensive exploration of spirituality in its archetypal and primordial essence. In the various human attempts to unravel the intricacies of the spirit world – in bygone days and in the present time – might we not be experiencing a primitive desire for like to connect with like? Is spirit more fundamental to our reality and existence than even body? Could it be that the human desire to engage with spirit is itself a dimension of universal global life? Perhaps, the spirit world is more about the world in its essential meaning, uncovering the primary spiritual nature of everything that exists, including creation itself – the primary, spiritual source, from which all creatures, including humans, inherit the capacity to act and respond in a spiritual manner.

When we refer, therefore, to the spirit world, we are not inferring that spirit-beings, divine or otherwise, arrive on earth from some other supernatural realm. We are alluding, first and foremost, to the realm of creation itself, as being fundamentally the domain of spirit. The primary and overwhelming data of creation is the creative vacuum, a seething conundrum of spiritual energy birthing forth life in the vast array of life-forms, from galaxies to human beings. In itself the creative vacuum is not a proof for the existence of God, a theological issue that is not of immediate concern for spirituality. What it does bear evidence to is a prodigious fertility and creativity far beyond anything we humans could produce or make possible.

Re-awakening our spiritual vision

Most people who talk and write about spirituality do so in reference to human beings alone. The notion that other creatures might be spiritual in some sense is not a consideration entertained by mainstream spiritual traditions.

Nor do we consider the Earth or the cosmos to be spiritual in any serious sense, certainly not on par with the spiritual capacity of human beings. Our spirituality is incarcerated in a dangerous ideology of self-inflation. We have set rigid human boundaries on what is essentially a radically creative life-force; the more we try to hem it in, as we have been doing for the past few thousand years, the more we end up producing an idolatrous monster, made in our own image and likeness.

Ironically, the redemption of spirituality is likely to emerge from where we would least expect: from the creation itself, especially as we relate with its daily impact in our capacity as earthly, planetary creatures. In this encounter, we begin to come home to our true selves, as the progeny of a reality greater than ourselves, without which our lives are seriously deprived of meaning and purpose. As we reconnect with the cosmic womb of our being and becoming, we will rediscover that our spiritual hunger is itself an expression of a sacred life-force, animating planet and universe alike. It is not we who make creation holy or sacred; rather, we are endowed with an innate yearning for spiritual wholeness because that happens to be the fundamental essence of the planet and universe we inhabit.

In recent decades, perhaps the strongest evidence for the fundamental spiritual nature of universal and planetary life comes, not from some radically new insights into the religions, nor from the scholarly deliberations of theologians, but from the profoundly transforming experiences of the astronauts viewing planet Earth from outer space. When we can perceive reality from within the big picture, we see things in a different light; and perhaps there is something more of the power of the creative vacuum that impacts upon us when we move in the realms of outer space. The reflections and impressions of the astronauts are often quoted in spiritual literature; the following is a brief sample:

> I love looking on the Earth. It isn't important whose she is, just that she is.
>
> *Oleg At'kov (USSR)*

> Seeing the Earth for the first time, I could not help but love and cherish her.
>
> *Taylor Wang (China)*

On the return trip home, gazing through 240,000 miles of space toward the stars and planet from which I had come, I suddenly experienced the universe as intelligent, loving and harmonious. My view of the planet was a glimpse of divinity.

Edgar Mitchell (USA)

You realise that on that small spot, that little blue and white thing, is everything that means anything to you – all of history and music and poetry and art and death and birth and love, tears, joy, games, all of it on that little spot out there. You recognise that you are a piece of that total life. . . . And when you come back there is a difference in that world now. There is a difference in that relationship between you and that planet and you and all those other forms of life on that planet, because you have had that kind of experience.

Russell Schweickart (USA)

I really believe that if the political leaders of the world could see their planet from a distance, their outlook would be fundamentally changed. . . . I think the view from 100,000 miles could be invaluable in getting people together to work out joint solutions, by causing them to realise that the planet we share unites us in a way far more basic and far more important than differences in skin, colour, or religion, or economic system. . . . If I could use only one word to describe the Earth as seen from the moon, I would ignore both its size and colour and search for a more elemental quality, that of fragility. The Earth appears fragile above all else. I don't know why, but it does.

Michael Collins (USA)

These are the reflections and responses of people whose inner spiritual centres are tuned in to the spirit at work in the creation itself. They all refer to the Earth as if it is a living organism, a view which modern science is reluctantly entertaining as valid and useful. Many of the quotes refer to Earth as a female, evoking sentiments expressed by adherents of the Great Goddess worship. And for each of those astronauts their hearts are changed; something very deep in their primal awareness has been touched afresh. And they know, in a way that words could never express, that they have glimpsed something of the power and beauty of divine life itself.

They have made a unique contribution towards '. . . raising the spiritual to the level of the obvious' (Chittister, 1995, p. 24).

The astronauts will not need to engage in a seance or in some modern esoteric ritual to make contact with the spirit world. For them, the spirit world is much more about the benevolent creative Spirit that inhabits and enlivens creation as they experienced it from the space journey. For them proof of a spirit world is irrelevant, even meaningless; nor do they feel any urge to analyse what the spirit world is all about; that would almost be a form of blasphemy! The experience itself is worth more than all the proofs or explanations that could ever be furnished. The encounter of spirit with spirit carries its own rationale, an engagement that is in no way alien to either human or earthly life but one that leaves an indelible impression on the human heart along with the conviction of the ultimate unity and meaning of all that exists.

A Spirit-filled universe

The spirit world that concerns us in this book is not that of strange, mysterious encounters between humans and some type of superhuman beings (ghosts, poltergeists, spirit-guides, etc.). These realities merit study and consideration in their own right; in my opinion, they comprise just one dimension of a far more comprehensive reality related not just to humanity but to creation at large. Creation itself is impregnated with spirit power, illustrated comprehensively in the work of Swimme & Berry (1992); the driving force of evolution is inherently creative, fuelled by the erotic energy of passion, intimacy and meaning.

The fundamental elements of nature, subatomic substances known as quarks, function in a relational mode and can only be comprehended and studied in a relational context. Scientists have never succeeded in isolating a quark or in substantiating its identity as an isolated building block. Aided by more powerful particle accelerators, they believe and hope that, one day, they may succeed in isolating and splitting the quark (more on this topic in *New Scientist*, 10 July 1993). Meanwhile, in their compulsion to divide and conquer, the scientists are in danger of missing the more fundamental truth staring them in the face: nature is not about isolated building blocks, but about patterns of interrelating and benevolent energy.

It is something of that same inherent spirit-force that creates and maintains the complex and mysterious interaction of the four forces of nature: gravitation, electro-magnetism, the strong and the weak forces. Gravitation is a particularly fascinating phenomenon, repelling and attracting the various bodies that comprise the known physical world. And all these forces operate within a time-space curvature, which because of its curved nature pushes everything towards interdependence, interaction and mutuality. According to Swimme & Berry (1992, p. 77), alienation for a particle is a theoretical impossibility; could it be otherwise in a world nurtured and sustained by a benign spirit-force?

Contemporary spiritual writers (following in the vein of Nouwen, 1986 and Rolheiser, 1979) devote much attention to the contemporary sense of human alienation. They tend to situate the problem within the human heart itself, giving only marginal and superficial attention to the world we humans inhabit. Karl Marx provides a much more holistic analysis of human alienation for which he traces four chief causes:

1. Human subjects are estranged from their products.
2. There is no intrinsic satisfaction from work.
3. Humans become estranged in their social relationships.
4. Humans fail to fulfil their nature as 'species beings'.

We are creatures of context, whose essential life and meaning belongs to a spiritual relational matrix requiring nothing less than the entire planet (and possibly the entire universe) to realise its full potential. It is because we are so alienated from our cosmic, planetary womb, and from our own species (as Marx highlights) that we feel such ennui – and not merely because we are out of tune with our inner selves.

It is the process of evolution itself, rather than any set of human experiences, that lies at the heart of our spiritual story. Out of the primordial silence, there irrupted a massive, explosive burst of energy, which we now call the Big Bang. Where it came from remains, and probably always will, the eternal enigma for some, the eternal mystery for others. It seems important to note that it came out of silence, a quality of nothingness that contained the raw potential for the elegance and creativity we see all around us.

In the beginning was silence, and not something akin to sound, as many of the great religions suggest. Spirit is at its best in silence, a quality of presence that underpins and pre-dates all forms of sound, an energy that embraces a potency, which Christians and others describe as the creative power of God. The fact that such enormous power can emerge from silence is itself a pointer to the fact that life's richest and deepest experiences will tend to be couched in paradox. Rational and patriarchal cultures cannot stomach paradox because it strives to keep open possibilities that our controlling culture perceives as threatening and dangerous.

And this is precisely our difficulty with an experience like that of the Big Bang: instead of striving to be open and receptive to its volatile, spiritual power we strip it of mystery and beauty by trying to analyse and control its every movement and dimension. Fortunately, as we scan the aeons of evolution's trajectory, as outlined by spiritual visionaries like Swimme & Berry (1992), we can scarcely avoid the conclusion that something quite special is at work here. Occasionally that leads to speculations that begin to embrace a spiritual *raison d'être* and are occasionally expressed in statements like: 'The God-idea does not stand above and outside of evolution as an ethical norm, but in true mysticism is placed into the unfolding and self-realisation of evolution' (Jantsch, 1980, p. 308).

Science now understands our world – in both its nature and evolution – as being endowed with an enormous capacity for self-renewal. It is this growing awareness that we inhabit and belong to a self-organizing universe that provides the most impressive evidence for a spirit-filled world. Our most immediate evidence is that collated by advocates of the Gaia hypothesis (Lovelock, 1979, 1988), highlighting the several delicate balances that exist in the biochemical make-up of planetary life, pointing to the conclusion that the planet itself seems capable of adjusting its resources when its viability is under threat.

This autopoietic propensity is characteristic not merely of planet Earth, but of the entire evolutionary process; this is elegantly demonstrated in the oxygen crisis of some four billion years ago. Today, we breathe oxygen as an essential life-sustaining element, but when it first evolved, oxygen was pure poison and killed off the existent life-forms of the time, mainly algae and various bacteria. To counteract the destructive power of oxygen, evolution evoked a totally new creative response which today we call respiration (the ability to breathe). In this way the deadly enemy was transformed into one of life's greatest allies and support systems. It was the creation itself, with its innate self-organising, spiritual power that brought about the transformation; in fact, creation is doing this all the time, often to rectify the damage caused by the alien and alienating behaviour of intruders like us, human beings.

Perhaps the hardest lesson for us to learn is that the spiritual impetus of evolution and creation thrives on a logic bigger and deeper than anything our minds are capable of comprehending. Central to these dynamics is the notion of paradox (Handy, 1994). Evolution does not unfold in a sequential, linear succession of events, but in quantum leaps often fuelled by what seems a crazy logic to human understanding. For example, many of the great outcomes of the evolutionary process emerge from chaos or destruction. Great breakthroughs are often preceded by mass extinctions, some of which seem to have lasted for millions of years (more on this topic in Leakey & Lewin, 1996).

Destruction seems to be the handmaid of creation, a paradox that underpins so much transformation and growth in the plant and animal world. A life-force is at work, and has been for billions of years, that behaves in a strangely baffling way; yet, it seems to know what it is about. As we view evolution on the grand scale, we are left in no doubt that there is a sense of direction, a growth in complexity, a sense of purpose underpinning it all (not necessarily an ultimate goal towards which the whole process is directed).

Not only on the grand scale, but frequently, too, in front of our very eyes, in daily events and experiences that no longer enthral us because we are so out of touch with our contemplative intuition which is what always connects us to the deeper meaning. Take this description offered by the sociobiologist, Edward O. Wilson (1992, p. 329):

> Organisms are all the more remarkable in combination. Pull out the flower from its crannied retreat, shake the soil from the roots into the cupped hand, magnify it for close examination. The black earth is alive with a riot of algae, fungi, nematodes, mites, springtails, enchytraeid worms, thousands of species of bacteria. The handful may be only a tiny fragment of one ecosystem, but because of the genetic codes of its residents it holds more order than can be found on the surfaces of all the planets combined. It is a sample of the living force that runs the earth – and will continue to do so with or without us.

The universe knows what it's about and the universe does not seem to have a problem about that. We do have a problem about it all; could it be that in fact it is we ourselves who are the real problem?

To resolve humanity's problem – which is still the misguided attempt to conquer and control the entire universe – we need to rediscover afresh what it means to inhabit a planet and a universe alive with the power of spirit, a mode of being and becoming which we can only encounter and appreciate by reappropriating our spiritual identity. And to do that we will need to divest ourselves of so much we have taken for granted, considered to be unquestioned and insuperable, including a great deal of irrelevant (and irreverent) baggage that belongs to the age of formal religion.

Our spiritual vision, inherited from official religion or from the spiritual traditions of the past few thousand years is not merely inadequate; it may, in fact, be a great delusion, based on the inflated, patriarchal instinct of a power-crazy species. We need to shed the whole thing, with its trappings of dogmas, rituals, laws and regulations. And as we seek to retrieve the deeper tradition, particularly if we feel the need to remain within the tradition, we will need to liberate ourselves from our slavery to orthodoxy in order to imbibe the deeper mystical wisdom that tends to irrupt in the unexpected realms of our daily life and experience.

More importantly, however, is the need to reconnect with the spiritual impetus of evolution itself, the unfolding cosmic drama in which spirit begets life in abundance, enlivening our weary hearts and re-awakening our petrified imaginations. And let's liberate ourselves from the self-righteous procrastinators who seek to guard the gates of the spiritual realm, blind to the fact that they have tightly locked those gates many thousands of years ago. These are the ardent 'evangelists' who forever warn us against the dangers of 'dabbling' in spiritual matters; because they don't know how to handle such realities, they assume we don't know either. But that is their short-sightedness, based on their alienation from the creative God whose Spirit blows where s(he) wills, endowing creation with the divine flame which human anthropocentricism can never extinguish.

In fact, most humans have not tried to extinguish the spiritual flame. Despite all the interference and manipulation of religious imperialism, the search for authentic spirituality weaves its own dynamic web, era in, era out. Ours is a great spiritual story, a tradition that pre-dates by thousands of years the rise of the formal religions. In this time of transition, it is eminently important for humanity and for planet Earth that we reconnect with that Sacred Epic. We begin to do so in the next chapter.

— 4 —

Reconnecting with our
spiritual tradition

The word 'sacred' like the words 'power' and 'medicine' has a very different
meaning to tribal people than to members of technological societies. It does not
signify something of religious significance . . . but something filled with an
intangible but very real power of force, for good or bad.

Paula Gunn Allen

The Body is the very universality of things. . . . My matter is not a part of the
universe that I possess totally. It is the totality of the universe that I possess
partially.

Teilhard de Chardin

THE AFRICAN MYTHOLOGIST, Malidoma Patrice Some
(1993) bemoans the loss of tradition in our Western lifestyle,
and with it an inability to engage in meaningful ritual. Tradition
has quite an ambiguous meaning in our world today. While African
peoples honour the tradition of the ancestors over many thousands
of years, in the West we tend to equate tradition either with the
'civilisation' of the past 5,000 years or the traditions relating to our
different religious systems spanning the past 4,500 years. Sometimes the word is used to describe events and experiences that
might be little more than 100 years old.

How we interpret tradition presents even greater problems.
There are those who wish to discard outrightly anything that
'belongs to the past'. There are others, particularly those who rely
heavily on religious meaning, who believe that tradition should
never be tampered with. A more enlightened minority argues that
if our inherited wisdom is not reinterpreted, on a regular basis,
automatically it becomes a dead tradition, and potentially a dangerous ideology.

As already highlighted, virtually all discourse about spirituality
assumes the 2,000 years of Christianity to be the tradition underpinning our lived practice. Obviously adherents of other religious

traditions will differ, and opt for their own 'closed' system. It is precisely this closed-system thinking that continues to undermine the meaning and task of spirituality in today's world.

Tradition expanded

In this book, I wish to adopt an enlarged horizon of tradition which will attempt to include:

1. The fact that creation itself is essentially spiritual and has been since its origins, with the divine life-force co-creating with the multiplicity of unfolding life-forms.
2. That humans since their first moments of evolution have engaged with a spiritualised universe, themselves endowed with a spiritual capacity for such engagement.
3. That we, humans, have prayed and worshipped in a conscious and enlightened way for at least 70,000 years, long before formal religions were heard of.
4. That for much of the Paleolithic era (c. 40000–10000 BCE), we engaged universally in a sophisticated and highly creative form of spiritual unfolding centred on the Great Mother Goddess.

To ignore or bypass any one of these elements does a fundamental injustice to our spiritual tradition as a human species. To ignore all these elements (or virtually ignore them) desecrates our spiritual heritage, impoverishes our spiritual meaning, ridicules our spiritual story, and alienates us from the fundamental identity that has been ours not just for thousands, but for millions of years. To retrieve and reclaim our sacred tradition, in its full evolutionary and cultural grandeur, is one of the most urgent tasks of our time. Anything short of this, only adds to the sense of ennui and betrayal that is felt by the millions who suffer from the spiritual suffocation of the past few thousand years.

Paleontologists believe that humans have inhabited planet Earth for at least four million years (4.4 million according to the American anthropologist, Tim White). *Homo erectus* seems to have come on the scene about two million years ago and *homo sapiens* – with virtually all the endowments we possess today – has been around for an estimated 200,000 years.

It is only in the past 100 years that we have been able to piece together something of what life was like for our ancient ancestors. Judging by customs and mores of extant tribal groups, ethnologists and anthropologists deduce what life must have been like for our 'primitive' forebears. Words like primitive, prelogical, preliterate, crude, savage, cannibalistic occur frequently in the scientific literature. Compared with us, as we are now in our 'civilised' world, these ancient peoples had a long way to go and a great deal to learn.

As time advances, tools of investigation become more thorough and refined, perceptions change and ideological viewpoints are challenged and reassessed. Discoveries in archaeology are particularly pertinent to force reassessment even of the most dogmatic position. Take for instance, the unquestioned priority of 'man the hunter' which we now perceive in a different light:

A salient characteristic of the 'man the hunter' theory is that it proposes that the bonding that led to the creation of the first human communities was bonding between males to more successfully hunt. However, as many scientists have now pointed out, hunting is hardly a major activity among nonhuman primates. Nor was it among early hominids; fossil remains indicate that (like apes and monkeys) they too survived primarily on a vegetarian diet. In fact even for contemporary foraging societies, the majority of calories usually come from food that is gathered – so much so that the anthropologist Ashley Montagu argues that they should properly be called gathering-hunting rather than hunting-gathering. While meat from big game is valued, the primary diet is composed of vegetables and fruits, as well as very small sources of animal protein, such as snails or frogs. So in its most basic premises, the 'man the hunter' theory of hominid and early human social organization rests on very shaky ground. (Eisler, 1995, p. 38)

And as we confront our current world-view with its enormous potential for barbarity and destruction, we are often forced to acknowledge that the 'noble savage' of ancient times was not as primitive a creature as we one time assumed. Consequently, scholars such as Lucien Levy Bruhl have had to revoke their attribution of prelogical and Max Muller's belief that myth was really a 'disease of language' is no longer accepted even by conservative scholars.

Reclaiming our spiritual tradition

It was the discoveries of Ice Age art, initially in the caves of Lascaux (France) and Altamira (Spain), that alerted scholars to the creative potential of our ancient ancestors. Already 35,000 years ago, we encounter a highly developed spiritual and artistic imagination characterised by depths of intuition and understanding that amaze and baffle even our own contemporaries. And when we combine these findings with the more recent discoveries at Catal Huyak (in Turkey), confirming the elaborate and widespread worship of the Great Mother Goddess for some 35,000 years (40000–5000 BCE), we realise that we are dealing with issues of immense spiritual and theological import.

The more we discover, the more we realise that this ancient tradition is an integral dimension of our spiritual story as a human species, a story that is deeply ingrained in our collective psyche, a narrative that informs so much of the spiritual search which people pursue today. Currently, we date the first concrete evidence for a spiritual dimension in humans to 70000 BCE. This, so far, is our earliest dating of ancient burial customs which reveal a distinctive sense of ritual and spiritual intent. In laying their dead to rest, our ancestors believed they were engaging with other life-forms, different from their own, yet very real and capable of affecting, for will or for woe, the exigencies of life here on Earth. They regarded such spirit-creatures with a mixture of awe and trepidation; the evidence seems to suggest that they considered them to be basically benign and benevolent.

Studies on our development as spiritual people in prehistoric times suggest that animism is one of the earliest forms of religious belief (a thesis first propounded by E. B. Tylor in 1871). According to this explanation our ancestors would have attributed the movement of water, the energy in fire and the power in wind to a 'soul' which inhabited these forces. The soul itself was considered to be the chief characteristic of a personalised spirit which inhabited the whole of creation, for which R. R. Marett coined the term 'Mana' in 1900. (Some scholars consider Mana to be an impersonal rather than a personalised force.)

Subsequently, magic became one of the better-known ritualistic practices adopted by our ancestors to access the divine power. In his famous thirteen-volume study, *The Golden Bough*, James G.

Frazer claims that magic precedes religion, suggesting an evolution from an inferior mode to a more enlightened one. Few anthropologists today would concur with this appraisal; instead they tend to view magic and religion as two ways of interpreting the universe in the human attempt to grapple with the encompassing mystery of existence (e.g. Ruth Benedict and Claude Levi-Strauss).

By the same token, the tendency to view magic as an attempt to control and manipulate reality, drawing evidence from contemporary tribal practices (as adopted by Barnes, 1984, pp. 200ff.) is a methodology that no longer commands widespread credibility. The urge to control and manipulate reality, as expressed in the contemporary world – by tribal peoples or in the population generally – is an inference of the patriarchal will-to-power which did not prevail with equal virulence in prehistoric times. Devoid of this patriarchal influence, ancient magical customs probably had more to do with a mutual engagement with reality rather than an attempt to exert control over it.

There are other ancient religious practices, such as witchcraft, totemism, shamanism, divination, and several forms of sacrifice, which merit a fresh evaluation. Witchcraft is a progeny of magic with a distinctive focus on healing and human well-being. Still widely practised in parts of Africa (despite missionary and colonial attempts to suppress it), it adopts a range of contemporary forms (e.g. covens) celebrating human or planetary fertility and healing. Elements of shamanic ecstasy and sacrificial practices often accompany contemporary forms of witchcraft.

Totemism occurs regularly in the study of ancient religion; and for the sociologist, Emile Durkheim, the totem is a religious emblem of central importance, as he perceived among the Australian aborigines. Totemism is rooted in the belief that members of a clan or tribe are united by kinship to some animal or plant from which they are descended. The totem is considered to be a sacred being, benevolent and helpful to humans. Ritually, the clan celebrates its common unity and allegiance in ceremonially consuming the blood of the totem animal, a possible prototype for the notion of religious sacrifice. Once again, we encounter patriarchal overtones, linking totemism almost exclusively with the origin of religion rather than considering it to be a stage in the development of religious consciousness.

Before we can fully engage with the deeper meaning of these

ancient practices, we need to strip away the veneer of formal religion, along with its accompanying ritual and worship, from which standpoint we tend to judge (usually misjudge) the significance of this archaic tradition. We also need to divest ourselves of the patriarchal framing with its compulsive urge to structure everything (including spirituality) in a manner that suited the masculine will-to-power, along with the sinister desire to undermine the spiritual power of the feminine that prevailed in previous millennia (more on this in subsequent chapters). A whole new set of perceptions is required if we are to discern authentically the meaning and spiritual impact of this ancient tradition. According to Leeming & Page (1994, p. 10):

> It seems likely that worship as we know it would have been unnecessary for a people who were not separate from their source, who like the trees, the animals and everything else on Earth – were emanations of the Goddess. Goddess as understood by these ancient people was clearly an immanent rather than a transcendent expression of the Great Mystery of life. She was no hidden sky deity; she was present in every aspect of the pulsating and cyclic existence of which humankind, her organ of consciousness, was aware.

We need to remind ourselves frequently that formal religion is a very recent visitor to planet Earth, no more than 5,000 years old; its significance will be explored in the next chapter. What emerged in the pre-religious era, our central concern in this chapter, can neither be gleaned, evaluated nor appreciated by using religion as a sole or main guideline. We are dealing with something fundamentally different, a primal experience that permeates created reality, and especially our humanum, in its essential nature, in a manner far exceeding, in depth and quality, anything religion has ever tried to achieve. We are engaging with something akin to what Moore (1993) calls the power of soul. We are dealing with a search for meaning that is imprinted – first and foremost – in the fabric of creation itself and becomes conscious in the dreams and aspirations of the human heart.

For a start, we need to transcend the castigations which our so-called civilised world attributes to our ancient ancestors, relegating to the realms of darkness, ignorance and paganism, a spiritual yearning that was probably every bit as authentic for its own time as contemporary expressions are for ours. As already indicated, we can no longer discern the true meaning of ancient practices by reviewing behaviour patterns of currently extant tribal groups; externally and superficially, behaviours may seem alike, but at all times in history the contemporary consciousness affects attitudes and behaviours to a degree not easily quantified or measured with the tools of rational science. Contemporary tribal groups, despite their apparent links with ancient ways of life, belong to the present time (and not to the ancient past) and are deeply affected by contemporary culture.

At home with nature

One of the outstanding features of our ancient ancestors – an archetypal yearning of the heart very much in vogue today – was their interdependence with nature. For most of our evolutionary time, we humans were a planetary rather than a national people. We lived in unison with planet Earth as our cosmic home, and increasingly the evidence suggests that we felt very much at home in the planet. The anti-world spirituality of recent millennia was unknown for most of that time. The whole planet was ours to roam wheresoever we wished. Whether on land or on sea, we belonged to a reality greater than ourselves, an entity that nourished and sustained us in our daily being.

Long before the Gaia hypothesis was formulated (Lovelock, 1979, 1988), our ancient ancestors seemed to possess an intuitive sense of an alive planet. They discerned in the forces of nature a power (mana), at once awesome and wonderful, and occasionally frightening, a life-force that impacted upon their daily lives. Whether this was a personal or impersonal force did not preoccupy our ancestors as it preoccupies us today; dualistic distinctions were largely unknown in this ancient culture. The life-force communicated primarily through the felt energies of nature: the warmth of the sun; the brightness of the moon; the flow of water; the productivity of earth; the rage of fierce storms; the serenity of a golden sunset; the inner powers of the human psyche which both the magician and the witch of old discerned as being interconnected with an energy greater than its own. The people acknowledged the nearness of the divine power and worshipped it in a series of rituals focused on the moon, the sun or the fertility of nature itself.

And from this nature worship there emerged a sense of cycle and rhythm: the beginning and end of day; the interaction of light and darkness; the rise and ebb of the tides; the cyclic dimensions of life (menstruation, fertility, etc.), the seasonal structure of time. A sense of purpose clearly prevailed; all indications are that these peoples did not feel the ennui and alienation often experienced in today's world.

The secret to this ancient sense of harmony seems to be that of an intuitive interdependence of spirit with spirit. The spirit within and the spirit without were in tune. Deep within the human psyche – at all stages of our evolutionary development – is a power of spirit seeking engagement and expression. Deep within creation itself is the same creative spirit. We don't have to be baptised, confirmed or ritualised in any sacramental experience to become aware of, and engage with, this spiritual wellspring. It is a natural, divine endowment. It is both the essence of our humanity and the power for engagement that grounds us in our planetary and cosmic reality as a human species.

Our social and cultural dislocation in today's world is based on our alienation of spirit. We have lost touch with the spirit within and correspondingly with the spiritual power that surrounds us. We are out of tune with the fundamental nature of life, our own and that of our universe. We are haunted by a sense of 'cosmic homelessness' (Haught, 1993, esp. pp. 39–65), an uprooted and dislocated people torn and tossed by the superficial values of consumerism, progress, exploitation and insipid religiosity. And the more we try to rectify our problem – by anthropocentric interference, scientific certitude or religious dogmatism – the more desperate our situation becomes.

Our sin of disconnectedness

We need to reconnect with the cosmic and planetary womb that begets, sustains and nourishes us. To dismiss worship of the sun, moon or elements of nature as 'primitive, pagan practices' highlights the appalling spiritual ignorance of 'civilised' humanity rather than the (mis)perceived naïvety of our ancient ancestors. It misses the deeper meaning: the capacity to transcend, the exploration of meaning, the pursuit of ultimacy, the articulation of inter-relatedness, inherent to both humanity and creation at large. It misses the overwhelming impact of our spiritual endowment (in both its light and its shadow).

When we become disconnected from our primal, spiritual roots – which is frequently what formal religions, especially the monotheistic ones, seek to do – we behave in strange and frightening ways; we behave in a dis-spirited way; we become belligerent and moody like alienated adolescents (cf. Sahtouris, 1989); the head and the heart move in opposite directions, detrimental to both, and to everything else we engage with in our daily lives.

Our disconnectedness is very much the product of our misguided progress, under the detrimental influence of patriarchal interference. In order to undermine the matristic culture of ancient times, with its governing Goddess patronage, the forces of patriarchy sought to separate humans from their close connectedness with nature and thus, in due course, set up an antagonistic relationship with the natural world. This move culminated in a series of anthropological and psychological theories which to this day tend to equate our relationship with the planet as that of a child to its parents, particularly to its mother.

Maturation, therefore, involved extricating oneself from anything that might smack of dependence on all those external factors that impinge upon human meaning and human well-being. Thus we arrive at the concept of the robust individual, autonomously independent, self-sufficient, highly skilled, capable of competing at any game, a 'self-made man'. It is an impressive mask behind which hides many a lonely soul, many an alienated spirit, many a brutal tyrant, many a cruel manipulator, many a false God!

Our prehistoric experience, with its variegated growth and development over some 70,000 years, is a stark reminder of how disconnected we have become as a human species and the brutalities we have wrought in the name of such disconnectedness. We have betrayed that innate nurturing, spiritual wisdom that has sustained us through the millennia. But much more serious is the disassociation (and consequent dislocation) of spirituality from its divine evolutionary context.

Spirituality is written into the weaving and unweaving tapestry of evolution and creation. Our prehistoric ancestors behaved spiritually because they remained connected to the cosmic womb of life, which itself is innately spiritual. And it is only by reconnecting with that primordial source – as millions are striving to do today (often in confusing and contradictory ways) – that we can hope to regain our spiritual, planetary and cosmic dignity as a human species. The divine meaning of creation is not derived from us, humans; creation itself is the source and wellspring; we, humans, are the derivative species!

The spiritual story itself is much more powerful and coherent than any text-book definition or description of spirituality. When we reconnect with that source of pregnant meaning we come to understand the yearnings of the past which are also the ones that arise spontaneously in our hearts today. We reconnect with that inner, vital, divinely-bestowed energy that drives us towards a sense of purpose and meaning in our lives, in the process of which we seek to transcend the immediate boundaries of our here-and-now experience. Four key words will help us to engage with that experience and explore its deeper significance: meaning, ultimacy, transcendence, and relatedness.

The search for meaning

We, humans, cannot tolerate meaninglessness for very long. Something deep within compels us to seek meaning and to 'invent' it when it is not readily available or when other forces militate against it (i.e. torture, sickness, etc.). The urge to meaning is primal (as in the infant's desire for the breast), prelogical, subconscious, fundamental to the very essence of human existence, just as it is central to the unfolding of cosmic evolution itself. It is the over-riding governing force behind everything in being.

At the unconscious level, meaning also underpins a great deal of animal and bird behaviour, but without ever becoming conscious as happens to us, humans. At the conscious level, everything we humans undertake is fuelled by the instinct towards meaning, and that becomes apparent when we review and examine our motivations. George Kelly of the Personal Construct school of psychology one time described suicide as the last desperate attempt at meaning in a world that had become totally meaningless. The most bizarre and destructive forms of human behaviour are governed by a desire and yearning for meaning. We cannot avoid searching for meaning, nor can we diminish our insatiable yearning for it.

Almost in spite of ourselves we search out a life governed by significance and a sense of purpose, but because we are so out of touch with that fact (namely, our spiritual *raison d'être*) we pursue the search often in inappropriate, albeit highly destructive, ways. A first call to conversion for our time is to become aware – or in the great spiritual traditions of the East, become more enlightened. We need to come home to ourselves, befriend our inner reality, and learn once more what it means to be human which, as already indicated, requires a fresh appropriation of our planetary and cosmic identity.

Why is the search for meaning so enduring and incisive? Because meaning is ingrained in the very fabric of our being. Moreover, our destiny in life seems to have meaning built in to the very direction in which life and evolution carries us. Despite all the paradoxes and contradictions, deep within we know that that there is 'something more' to it all that defies all our logic and rational wisdom and is capable of transcending all the failures we encounter in our experience of the world.

The search for meaning has us hooked; it pursues us long after we have given up, or tried to make a convincing case for a world of total absurdity. It's not the case that we are afraid to face the utter grimness of an absurd world; our inability or unwillingness to engage with utter darkness is not escapist. It is often in the face of total meaninglessness that the urge to meaning takes on a grandeur defying all rationality (e.g., Victor Frankl). And some of the finest insights into the meaning of life have emerged from intense engagement with situations of utter meaninglessness. Ironically, it is sometimes when we refrain from imposing meaning, and choose instead to be totally present to our chaos and our darkness, that a strangely unexpected sense of meaning begins to emerge; one often experiences this while befriending people in the final hours of their earthly lives.

Philosophers, psychologists and spiritual writers often allude to meaning and our pursuit of it. Yet it remains something nebulous and marginal in both our awareness and educational systems. We do not take meaning seriously, and we are all the poorer for that. In a sense, we seem to collude with each other in perpetuating a myth of meaninglessness, and we endorse that collusive behaviour by devising and supporting a set of political, social and economic structures most of which are alien to human, planetary and cosmic well-being; little wonder that we have turned ourselves and our world into such a crazy place!

As a species we have become so uprooted and disconnected from our primal and prehistoric origins that we now behave in a manner which is destructive not merely of planetary life, but particularly to the destiny we set ourselves as a human family. If we feel alienated, as many do today, it is because we have deviated from our true nature and, consequently, created for ourselves a hell-on-earth! If our meaning has dried up, then it is we ourselves who have drunk the well dry. Could it be that we don't drink from the right wells anymore?

Ultimacy and transcendence

Ultimacy is not a word we use in daily discourse. It suggests a final point, place or purpose towards which everything moves or is destined to move. It can also be understood as the conviction that there is a purpose to what our lives are about; the journey leads somewhere, the precise nature of which may not be at all clear (and for some at least, unimportant).

A sense of the ultimate helps to keep reality open. It also helps to retain a sense of wonder, mystery and surprise. And above all it safeguards against the human will-to-power which seeks to dominate and control reality solely on human terms. In this way the human becomes a God unto itself, an anthropocentric form of idolatry that can be as stultifying and oppressive as any other humanly-based ideology.

The tendency towards such human domination, and the perceived rights of the human to exert power and control over other life-forms and the planet itself, is a relatively recent development in our evolutionary story. Of the 70,000 years of known spiritual development, it is only in the past 10,000 years that the will-to-power has been to the fore in human consciousness, spiritually and otherwise. Prior to 10000 BCE humans seem to have lived in a very different quality of rapport with the Earth, in a much more equalitarian, co-operative and spiritually-enlightened mode. The divine was perceived to be inherent to every aspect of life and there existed a widespread intuitive understanding that co-operation with the divine life-force was essential to meaningful life on Earth. In practically every dimension of their lives our ancestors lived in a transcendent mode.

In the contemporary literature on spirituality, transcendence is considered to be a central element. It denotes the openness and willingness to rise above our daily, mundane concerns in the acknowledgement that a life-force higher than us (which we tend to call God) influences and governs the course of events. Transcendence is not merely that realm of conviction and experience which keeps us open to the divine as beyond ourselves and our world; it is also the invitation to live and work in conjunction with that life-force which adds depth and meaning to our daily interactions within the world itself.

The words of the South African theologian, Albert Nolan (1988) are relevant and instructive:

> All these experiences of going beyond some limitation or restriction are experiences of God, because God is transcendence. God's voice is the call of transcendence that challenges us to go further, to do more, to try harder, to change our lives, to venture out into new areas and into the unknown. . . . God is out there calling us to move beyond the system, beyond sin, beyond suffering, beyond our narrow and limited ideas of what is possible.

Philosophical and spiritual texts tend to draw a sharp dictinction between immanence and transcendence. This smacks of dualistic opposition which is not merely unhelpful but may be dangerous and misleading. The distinction is often used by writers who seek to safeguard the 'beyondness' of God, the God of pure mystery who is radically above and beyond anything we can conceive or imagine. The concern seems stronger in the monotheistic religions, perhaps because they propagate various notions of the embodiment of God in our world, a feature that is most pronounced in the Christian conviction that God entered fully into our world as a human being like one of ourselves. The fear that we might immerse God too much in the world of our daily experience – the immanence – is itself based on an anthropocentric tendency to dictate who and what God should be for us.

It is at this juncture that we need to listen to and realign our consciousness with the evolutionary story so that we can learn from the rich and varied spiritual experiences of our ancestors over the millennia. Long before we coined words like immanence or transcendence, we experienced and worshipped God as both immanent and transcendent, and for thousands of years we had no problem with the integration of both dimensions. Obviously we cannot revert to this former way of engaging with our reality, but perhaps we do need to transcend the intellectual and linguistic quagmires which undermine rather than invigorate those experiences which touch so deeply into the meaning and purpose of our lives. Religion, in the very etymology of the word, is meant to link us into deeper meaning; what it often seems to exacerbate is the ossification of those very life-forces which should be the primary sources of our joy and liberation.

The capacity to relate

Many aspects of spirituality are construed in isolation and adversarially. We tend to juxtapose the sacred and the secular, the human and the divine, body and soul, religion and politics. Frequently, we need to remind ourselves that dualisms are constructs of the human mind (and of fairly recent invention) and do not necessarily reflect reality in its essential nature. There is overwhelming evidence – anthropological, scientific and spiritual – to suggest that life operates in terms of the both-and polarity rather than the either/or dualism.

While some division of labour – with respective male and female roles – seems to have existed among our prehistoric ancestors, there is nothing to suggest a dualistic vision of reality comparable to that of more recent times. The prevailing conviction of ancient times was that life is a unity, within which everything is inter-related and interdependent. Our ancestors did not worship the sun or moon in order to adore a higher being on whom they felt totally dependent; their worship was largely inspired by a keen awareness of the interdependence of all things. The sun was not some inanimate object up in the sky; it was something more akin to a friend who warms and nourishes us, a companion that needs to be befriended and thanked for its graciousness and generosity.

The capacity to relate may well be the most basic element of our spiritual make-up as a human species. Long before we learned to speak (about 100,000 years ago), humans related and inter-related with each other and with the universe they inhabited. The fact that we have related at a non-verbal mode for at least 90 per cent of our time on Earth is something we rarely advert to, and is a factor that impinges significantly upon our spiritual well-being at all stages of human evolution.

For most of our evolutionary history, we have been communicating and relating from the heart and gut rather than from the head. The predominance of cerebral, heady, linear logic in our contemporary way of being may have reached deleterious proportions; the head is in danger of outwitting the heart and the gut, and there is nothing in our evolutionary story to suggest the appropriateness of that development; in fact everything points to the need to keep the head subject to both the heart and the gut.[5]

It is difficult to identify the precise factors that enabled us to develop our capacity to relate as a human species. A co-operative inclination probably aided our survival more than a competitive or conflictual one, and the popular perception that our ancient ancestors were almost totally preoccupied with survival (and basically incapable of rising above that level of awareness) is a glaring example of the 'patriarchs of civilisation' projecting their dark and oppressive shadow onto the 'safe' scapegoats of bygone days. Could it be that we humans are more co-operative than competitive by nature? Could it be, as anthropological studies increasingly verify, that co-operation is more innate to our evolution than competition? Modern conditions don't substantiate that view, but we need to be careful not to judge everything by our contemporary status; one, as we'll indicate later, which is seriously flawed in several significant ways.

In the sacred evolutionary story, the discovery of fire must have been a moment of heightened spiritual and relational awareness for our ancient ancestors. Many anthropologists opt for the conservative dating for the discovery of fire as that of 300,000 years ago, drawing on evidence associated with Peking Man. Others are of the opinion that it probably dates back to 600,000 years ago, while Swimme & Berry (1992) date the discovery to 1.5 million years ago. Whatever the precise time, it does mark a significant shift in human consciousness, especially at the spiritual and relational levels. The connection with this new energy source, with its capacity to nourish, warm, bond and energise people, threw a whole new perspective on the meaning of life.

Gathering around the open fire, whether for cooking food, warming themselves or human friendship provides archetypal evidence for the tendency towards human community. It is in communing with each other, in the mutuality and sociality of the tribal moment, that new relational bonds are formed and cemented.

And we can surmise that it is from these fire-centred gatherings that the great spiritual and philosophical questions were first explored (at a non-verbal level), seeking the deeper meaning and purpose of existence. Long before ethical or moral guidelines were conceived, our ancient ancestors devised their own norms to live communally, integrally, and in harmonious interaction with the surrounding environment.

The capacity to relate – mutually and ethically – is innate to humanity itself; it is the central dimension of our spiritual repertoire. To quote Zappone (1991, p. 12):

> The pivotal shift in spirituality's meaning for the twentieth century resides in the birth of a worldview of interdependence or relationality. . . . In its broadest sense, spirituality centres on our awareness and experience of relationality. It is the relational component of lived experience. (emphasis mine)

Our whole understanding of what life is about is centred on the capacity to relate and the need to do so in mutually and spiritually beneficial ways. Any wonder then that one finds in practically all the great religious and spiritual traditions of humankind (with the notable exception of present-day Islam) a doctrine of the Trinity, the God we perceive to be primordially about inter-relatedness. Long before such a doctrine was developed in religious terms, it existed in the heart of the human community as a primal spiritual yearning (see Abraham, 1994; Miller, 1986). The trinitarian, relational God was at work in the people for millennia before theological or religious dogma was ever conceived.

Meaning, ultimacy, transcendence and relatedness characterise the spiritual unfolding of our species for some 70,000 years at a conscious level, and in the preconscious realm for possibly the two million years lifespan since our emergence as *homo erectus*. The more we delve into our ancient story as a human species what we tend to encounter is not the illiterate, cannibalistic savage, the projection of our own unintegrated shadow, but a creature spiritually and socially integrated with the evolving world of the time. It is this capacity to grow and unfold in conjunction with the larger evolving Earth-community (and cosmic community), in an inter-related and interdependent mode, that is at the heart of ancient spirituality. And it is this same spiritual hunger, focused on the inter-relationship of person-planet-cosmos that largely underpins the search for meaning – and for spirituality – in today's world as well.

All of which brings us to the burning question for contemporary spirituality: can we continue to assume that religion contributes positively and constructively to our evolution and development as spiritual beings? Is there not a growing (some would claim, over-whelming) body of evidence to suggest the opposite, namely that religion is a serious hindrance to the realisation, articulation and appropriation of our spirituality? Is religion outgrowing its spiritual usefulness? Is the age of formal religion coming to an end?

These are not just the questions of some weird, new-age atheist or agnostic. They are very real questions of our time, largely con-fined to the inner searchings of the human heart and rarely spoken aloud for fear of misunderstanding, harsh criticism or outright con-demnation. Pastorally, we tend to take such questions to the religious representatives of our culture (clergy, spiritual directors, theologians, etc.), but many of these people have a vested interest in maintaining the religious *status quo* – like the vicar in Ian's story (Chapter 1) – and because of their own spiritual and theological for-mation, may not be sufficiently receptive, vulnerable and informed to hear the echoes from the heart that accompany the spiritual search of our time.

When, where and why formal religion came into being is rarely addressed in the literature of spirituality. Without such redress, however, our attempts to explore a relevant spirituality for our time remain superficial and incomplete. In the next chapter, we review the growth and development of formal religion itself.

The shift from spirituality to religion

Historians have a responsibility to ensure that the historical perspective that they provide assists debate rather than serves a particular ideology . . . it is open to us to retrieve aspects of the past, long forgotten and even deliberately submerged, which may speak to us once again in the present.

Philip Sheldrake

Christianity, for the first time in its history, is faced with a large-scale challenge to the patriarchal interpretation of religion and an increasingly coherent vision of an alternative way of constructing the tradition from its roots.

Rosemary Radford Ruether

WHY DID WE LOSE THE CONNECTION with our ancient spiritual heritage? Why did we evolve religious systems that were intended to enhance our spiritual aspirations but in fact seem to have jeopardised – quite seriously – our spiritual development?

To address these questions we need to review a major shift in human consciousness that took place some 10,000 years ago, a development popularly known as the Agricultural Revolution, commencing around 8000 BCE and lasting down to about 1600 CE when the Industrial Revolution began to emerge. A great deal of research has been done on the Industrial Revolution and its impact – not merely on the West, but on the consciousness of our world generally. Now that the Industrial Age is diminishing (to varying degrees in different parts of the world), we find ourselves faced with questions which themselves are essentially spiritual, although rarely viewed in that light. Central to such questions, is the notion of the paradigm shift, about which much has been written in the past few decades (see Kuhn, 1970; Capra, 1982; Ó Murchú, 1992).

The shift ensuing with both the rise and fall of the Industrial Age merits much attention because its impact is so tangible and immediate. What many people don't realise is that the Industrial Age is

merely the 'icing on the cake' of the previous major shift known as
the Agricultural Revolution. Prior to the agricultural era, we lived
in close harmony with the Earth as one, unbroken reality. The earth
was experienced as a cosmic home, to which everybody belonged
and over which no one sub-group had control or exclusive dominion. Nor did humans feel any strong urge to master and control the
world. The Earth was understood to be a living organism, the
embodiment of the Great Mother Goddess, who nurtured and sustained life with prodigious fertility and overflowing abundance. It
would have been inconceivable that we should rupture the womb
that nourished us.

The Agricultural Revolution and the rise of patriarchy

Most researchers seem to underestimate the enormous impact of
the Agricultural Revolution, from both a planetary and human
viewpoint. Prior to that time, humans co-existed as one family; like
all other creatures, they understood themselves to be an integral
part of the one, unbroken reality. The current division of our planet
into what we now know as continental landmasses, nation states,
ethnic sub-groups and different religions was not merely unknown
in the pre-Agricultural era, but in fact was inconceivable. Separate
landmasses did exist, but even for the few who became aware of that
fact (through extensive travel) the separation was of no real significance, since land and sea were perceived as different dimensions of
the one underlying reality.

It is very difficult for us, and our contemporaries, to comprehend, never mind appreciate, the world-view of pre-Agricultural
times, and how this view influenced every aspect of human behaviour – always viewed in its relation to planetary life. Our desire to
understand is further impeded by centuries of patriarchal brain-
washing which tries to convince us that everything taking place
prior to the 'age of civilisation' (variously dated from c. 3000 BCE
until the present time) was primitive, barbaric, pagan, uncivilised.
Humankind had not come of age – according to our deluded, self-
inflated criteria – and consequently people could only behave in a
crude and animal-like fashion.

Frequently, these allegations, and the perceptions that accompany them, are projections from our barbaric present. We seek
scapegoats in our ancient past for those destructive and unpalatable

behaviours that we feel should not belong to a civilised people. In that way we don't have to confront the shadow of our personal and cumulative destructability; we find somebody else to blame for it – the ancient savages from whom we are all descended!

But who are the real savages? There is no evidence that our prehistoric ancestors murdered and maimed millions of innocent men, women and children to the extent that we have done in the warfare of the twentieth century. Nor is there anything to suggest in our ancient past a carved-up planet of haves and have-nots, where a minority gloat in wealth and obesity while an estimated three-quarters of humanity live on the verge of starvation. Nor did the so-called pre-literate peoples of bygone days pile up arms that could destroy planet Earth several times over. One of the major challenges of contemporary spirituality is the need to reclaim and deal with our collective shadow (more on this in Chapter 8). In fact, our choice not to do so almost certainly spells annihilation for *homo sapiens*. The time is fast appproaching when the insatiable urge to dominate and control, having destroyed much of the natural resourcefulness of the planet, is now precariously close to destroying ourselves also.

All of which seems to suggest that the Agricultural Revolution – and its subsequent developments via the Kurgan invasions – was a disaster for humankind. Like all major developments we are encountering light and darkness, and in the plan of universal life it seems we cannot have one without the other. The desire to advance the development and cultivation of the land gradually arose in human consciousness as hunting, tribal peoples traversed the planet and began to understand and realise its enormous potential to sustain and nourish life.

The Paleolithic era (c. 40000–10000 BCE) seems to have been one of favourable climatic conditions that produced rich vegetation and an abundance of food from the soil. And the accompanying spiritual consciousness, focused on the Great Earth Mother Goddess of prodigious fertility and sustenance, convinced humankind that it was only beginning to discover and appropriate the resources of the Earth. Thus there began to develop a more systematic programme of cultivation and farming, necessitating a certain division of labour and a portioning of the Earth to various sub-groups – probably along tribal lines.

The long-term benefits are well known. People grew into a

greater awareness and appreciation of the Earth's resourcefulness. Not alone was there greater abundance of food, and employment, but a growing awareness also that nature held many secrets to live healthily and to furnish a vast range of cures for various illnesses. Through the Agricultural Revolution humankind developed even a deeper sense that the planet was a supreme friend, always to be treated with gentleness, care, dignity and profound respect for its inherent laws and values. The concept of the Earth as a great nourishing mother became even more convincing and dominated the spiritual (and religious) consciousness until about 3000 BCE.

Meanwhile, the shadow side also gathers momentum, and with it some frightening and sinister developments (more accurately, deviations). The portioning out of land, while well intentioned, created a sense of possessiveness and greed. The more people were given, the more they wanted, and when they did not get it legally, they often claimed it by force. Tribal rivalries gradually assumed political status as land became a commodity for competition and aggrandisement. Thus was born the prototype of the nation-state, a concept totally unknown prior to this time. And as states became more autonomous and self-reliant, they also sought to conquer more and more land for their own wealth, comfort and self-inflation; thus were sown the seeds of modern warfare, another phenomenon unknown prior to the Agricultural Revolution.

Inventing the divine patriarch

From this time on, the force of law was based on the values of control and conquer, the supreme masculine, patriarchal motto that prevails unabated to our own time. And to validate that otherwise questionable ethic, the patriarchal male duly invented religion, projecting the image of a supreme male deity to match the supreme male conqueror on Earth. Could it be that we may be dealing with a more spurious and insidious development in the emergence of formal religions: the subconscious, if not conscious, attempt to control and conquer the divine power itself! Is religion the ultimate weapon of patriarchal dominion, rather than the benign revelation of a loving God?

In the Industrial Age, we sought to dominate the divine power by taking to ourselves the perceived role of God as the all-knowing being. By developing religious dogmatism, on the one hand, and scientific certitude on the other – and I wish to suggest that these two movements belong to the same subconscious will-to-power – we sought to make God redundant.

In the wake of the Agricultural Revolution, we adopted a different, but no less anthropocentric, approach. We conceptualised God in our own image and likeness as the Supreme Patriarchal Father, modelled according to the emerging cultural views of the time. The next misguided step was to assume that we could relate personally and intimately with that supreme being, which in due course justified us in becoming supreme ourselves. And from within this narcissistic will-to-power we ourselves began to play God. We invented a religious ideology to lord it over others as we envisaged God did and would always do.

In one sense this form of idolatry was even more blatant and destructive than that of the Industrial Age. In the latter, we tried to get rid of God by taking to ourselves the supreme wisdom of God; this often led to an agnostic rather than an atheistic stance, of the type one sometimes experiences in dialogue with mainstream scientists. What happened in the wake of the Agricultural Revolution was a highly convoluted form of idolatry, reducing, manipulating and distorting the God-reality into an impressive man-made idol, in whose name enormous pseudo-spiritual power was released to validate the human urge to dominate and control. We review briefly how this took place.

Around 4500 BCE, nomadic bands, sometimes described as the Eurasian Steppe Pastoralists, sought to obtain more fertile lands for their cattle-herds; they began to pursue their desires with a quality of invasion and barbarity largely unknown in previous times. Best known of these roving groups were the Kurgans of Eastern Europe, the Aryans in India, the Luwians in Anatolia, the Achaeans (and, subsequently, the Dorians) in Greece. Not long after, we notice the Hebrews in Canaan (Palastine) adopting a similar strategy, the destructive impact of which is well documented in the Hebrew scriptures (Old Testament).

The rather misleading term, Indo-European invaders, is often applied to this movement; others, like the anthropologist, Marija Gimbutas, tend to use the term Kurgan invaders and go on to describe three major strands: Kurgan wave No. 1, c. 4300–4200 BCE; wave No. 2, 3400–3200 BCE; wave No. 3, 3000–2800 BCE. Led by warriors and powerful priests, these invaders sought to justify their desire to conquer and control in the name of a male, con-quering God whom they sought to represent. With these invasions the image of the conquering chief on horseback becomes a preva-lent symbol adopted by both religion and politics for many subsequent centuries.

Human culture and civilisation as known up to this time changed dramatically, and apparently quite rapidly. The nature of that change is illustrated vividly by scholars such as Childe (1958), Gimbutas (1982) and Eisler (1987). To quote Gimbutas (p. 281):

> The old European and Kurgan cultures were the antithesis of one another. The old Europeans were sedentary horticulturalists prone to live in large well-planned townships. The absence of fortifications and weapons attests to the peaceful co-existence of this egalitarian civilisation that was probably matrilinear and matrilocal. The Kurgan system was composed of patrilineal, socially stratified, herding units which lived in small villages or seasonal settlements while grazing their animals over vast areas. One economy based on farming, the other on stock breeding and grazing, produced two contrasting ideologies. The Old Euro-pean belief system focused on the agricultural cycle of birth, death and regeneration, embodied in the feminine principle, a Mother Creatix. The Kurgan ideology as known from compara-tive Indo-European mythology, exalted virile, heroic warrior gods of the shining and thunderous sky. Weapons are non-existent in the old European imagery; whereas the dagger and battle-axe are dominant symbols of the Kurgans, who like all historically known Indo-Europeans, glorified the lethal power of the sharp blade.

Eisler (1987, esp. pp. 45–58) describes the destructive impact of the Kurgan invasions, not merely socially and politically, but spiritually also. A whole new attitude to life and its meaning came to the fore, and with it a subtle and sinister sense of divine power as predomi-nantly subjugating, invasive, destructive, patriarchal and warlike. And with these new developments came the gradual erosion, maybe even the deliberate subversion (as Eisler avers), of all that the cul-ture of the Great Mother Goddess signified. Woman, and all that woman-power symbolises, was to become the greatest victim of this upheaval, with consequences that prevail to our own time.

The spiritual undercurrents of the invading forces are central to the entire strategy. The strategy itself – divide and conquer – belonged initially to the shadow-side of the Agricultural Revolution; it was more a cultural rather than a religious phenomenon. Progressively, the religious motivation – focused on the supreme male conqueror, a projection of the male dominators themselves – becomes the overwhelming power fuelling the conquest and destruction. It was a short step, and indeed a short time, before this vision became a formalized religious system. It began to happen around 3000 BCE with the rise of Hinduism, and true to the spirit of 'divide and conquer' eventually evolved into a whole series of religious systems which to this day battle it out for the religious supremacy of the world.

The rise of formal religion

Religion in its more formal sense is very much a development of the past 5,000 years. Hinduism, whose origins are traced to the middle of the third millennium BCE, is considered to be the oldest of the formal religions. Prior to that time, worship and a religious value-system seems to have been extensively adopted but formal religions, as currently known (Hinduism, Buddhism, Christianity, Islam, etc.), did not exist.

The religions tend to be divided into two classes: polytheistic (belief in many Gods) and monotheistic (belief in one supreme God). Judaism, Christianity and Islam belong to the monotheistic category and pride themselves with a more mature, highly developed, and theologically more authentic view of God. Mainstream adherents of these religions use texts from their respective scriptures to justify and bolster this view, texts which allegedly contain the actual words of the supreme deity itself, e.g. 'I am the Lord your God, you shall not have false Gods before me' (Exod. 20; Deut. 5).

Such interpretation of sacred texts, often taking the words at their face value, is based on the assumption and conviction that the texts are divinely inspired and communicate the divine intent exactly as the divine power wishes. It seems to me that this entire argument is flawed, not so much with the primitive mythology that Rudolf Bultmann and others sought to correct with the process of dymythologisation, but with an anthropocentric arrogance that has outstretched all sense of limitation and is verging on pure idolatry.

Allowing for the fact that each of the religions is based on a gen-uine revelation from God, or from Gods – a fact which itself needs closer examination – the mode and extent in which we have received and accommodated that divine disclosure, says a great deal more about us, than it does about the divine. The whole process is riddled and convoluted with the imposition of the patriarchal, human urge to dominate and control reality.

The process whereby the mainstream religions came to be for-malised is very much based on the unquestioned assumption that God speaks as we speak, and acts as we act, and can be reduced to a system that we can not merely comprehend, but control in all its possibilities. Little wonder that, over the centuries, we have invoked God to justify anything from slavery, to apartheid, to human and earthly exploitation, even the catastrophic destruction of nuclear warfare.

The great Eastern religions retain – even to this day – a much more fluid and flexible notion of the divine power. Hinduism holds a belief in several Gods, ranging from those who exercise a univer-sal quality of influence to those who have a more distinctive significance for a particular person, place or object. Because Hin-duism is the oldest of the known religions, it retains something of the pluralistic flavour of pre-religious belief and its more amorphous and all-pervasive sense of the divine. Of interest, too, is the fact that Hinduism does not adopt (officially) a policy of proselytising (converting); it openly acknowledges the rightness and uniqueness of each system for its own adherents.

Buddhism, with an understandable unease about, and suspicion of, the Hindu proliferation of deities, goes to an opposite extreme, but one that perhaps should be viewed in complementary rather than in adversarial terms. It suspends the God question, inviting its adherents to 'let God be God', and instead devote their energy and commitment to the diminution and eradication of suffering in the world.

Judaism was the first of the monotheistic religions to evolve about 1000 BCE. Along with Christianity and Islam it prides itself in its belief in one true God, perceived to be superior in every sense to the many deities of other faiths. The patriarchal influence on the one hand, and the warrior-like figure of the Kurgan peoples on the other, are all too apparent in the monotheistic religions. To match and validate the power of the supreme human (usually the king or kuriarchial Lord), we evolved a set of belief systems in all of which the divine attributes are perceived and named as the qualities we desire most of all in the earthly, kingly rulers. Central to such kingship was the unique and unquestioned authority and power over all one's charges, human and otherwise.

In the long spiritual tradition of humankind, as outlined in previous chapters, there is little or no precedent for the patriarchal monotheistic embodiment of God. The whole story of evolution – on the universal, planetary and human scales – points unmistakably to a God who co-creates with all created reality. The God embodied in the era of the Great Mother Goddess is the God who continuously comes to birth in the explosion of supernovas on the one hand and in the blossoming forth of the tiny shoot on the other. The God to whom our ancient ancestors danced is the creative Spirit who blows in the wind, surges in the sea and impregnates in every coming-to-birth. It is the archetypal image of a God who is radically egalitarian and communitarian.

Divine revelation or human artefact

From an evolutionary and anthropological perspective, the image of the patriarchal, monotheistic God has all the tenor of another patriarchal artefact: dominant, oppressive, manipulative, male, judgmental and ruthless. In both Judaism and Christianity, these harsh qualities are toned down by invoking the notion of the Covenant: the relational God who seeks to enter into an egalitarian relationship with the people. Scholars in both traditions argue that this is the primary attribute of the God they seek to depict. Undoubtedly, this is true, not because scholars say it, but because the whole evolutionary story points towards it. In practice, however, it is not the Covenantal God who wins the day, but the harsh patriarchal judge, a fact that is all too apparent as we read through the respective histories of Judaism and Christianity alike.

Theologians and other scholars of religion work with many unexamined assumptions, notably that religion seems to be endowed with a type of eternal pre-existence making it the supreme primordial body of wisdom; that it is an authentically revealed form of divine wisdom – in fact that it is the only indisputable means that makes the divine revelation accessible to us; that religion is essential to any and every authentic form of spiritual life; that the capacity to transcend is impossible apart from faith based on formal religion; that religion enables people to develop a repertoire of symbols and rituals that facilitate a meaningful relationship with the divine on the one hand and with daily life on the other; that religion enforces a common will to meaning on the basis of which we can evolve relevant moral, social and political systems.

This line of argument is flawed on several levels, particularly in its apparent dismissal of the spiritual culture and aspirations of pre-religious times. God did not have to wait for formal religion to bring the divine power into the world; the divine co-creativity has been at work for billions of years and humans have been responding, on the overt level alone, for at least 70,000 years. The evidence we are rediscovering today, some of which has already been reviewed in this book, makes it abundantly clear that, comparatively speaking, the response of our prehistoric ancestors was every bit as authentic for their time, as ours is for this time.

The evidence pushes us further, however, and this is the conclusion that many do not wish to face: the ancient spiritual wisdom embraced our world in a holistic, organic way that mainstream religion does not seem capable of doing. Spirituality, in every age of human and planetary unfolding, is far more versatile, embracing, dynamic and creative than religion has ever been. Contrary to the major perceptions of religionists, spirituality, and not religion, is the primordial source of our search for meaning while also offering us a much more coherent route to a comprehensive experience of divine revelation.

Consequently, one of the major tasks for spirituality in this age, as in all others, is the prophetic challenge of confronting religion with its own shadow. Religion is not, and never has been, the primary mediating force for spirituality. Religion is not, and was never intended to be, the sole or primary medium for God's revelation to humankind. Religion is much more a human rather than a divine invention.

Historically and anthropologically, religion is so closely related to, and integrated with, the patriarchal urge to divide and conquer that it makes little sense apart from that specific cultural ambience. Religion belongs to an exaggerated perceptual view of reality wherein we tend to attribute to it eternal, primordial significance; in fact, it is a phenomenon with a life-span of about 5,000 years. We need to demolish, or at least reduce, the exaggerated, inflated image of religion, so that we can work at the retrieval of what really belongs to our evolutionary story as a human, planetary species, namely our interaction with, and relationship to, the co-creative God who is at the heart of spirituality but not necessarily at the heart of religion.

Religion has a shadow side

Although not extensively practised in the West, religion continues to exert a very strong influence on human life and culture, a great deal of which is negative and destructive. This can be most apparent when we review the impact of the religious shadow on human behaviour. Some people vociferously denounce religion and sometimes set in motion an anti-religious crusade; sometimes, these are people embittered by an emotional hurt arising from some destructive religious experience in the past.

People who disagree with the way a religion is lived or practised, are usually perceived as a threat; even if listened to, they are often left with the feeling that they have dabbled in something which really was none of their business. For that reason, most people who become disillusioned with religion, do not confront the pain or discomfort religion is causing them; they simply opt out. It is easier to move away rather than face the challenge, guilt and fear which the confrontation might involve.

Many of those who opt out, retain a strangely ambiguous respect for religion. For example in the social or political sphere they will never speak out against religion, and will at times take painstaking efforts to ensure that the religious side of the matter is handled by the 'experts' in that field, which tend to be the clergy; politicians often adopt this strategy.

Finally, there are those who may continue to practise, or have long abandoned such practice, but in either case remain full of guilt or shame, because of past moral transgressions or failure to live up to expectations. Religion inculcates in such people a perpetual state of fear and unworthiness.

All these scenarios represent something of the shadow side of formal religion, a realm of religious commitment that may have many more adherents than the sphere in which such belief is holistically and maturely integrated. We briefly review some of the outstanding features of the religious shadow:

1. *Fear.* All the religions claim to reveal a loving God, but in practice what they engender, often to the extent of psychological and
spiritual paralysis, is a crippling, destructive fear. Popular preaching and formal rituals exacerbate this fear by emphasising the
enormous gap between the all-perfect God and the imperfect
human being, who can never hope to attain union with that God
without a mysterious divine intervention. This fear often leads to
an internalised sense of oppression, a gnawing sense of unworthiness and occasionally feelings of insurmountable guilt.

Three dominant reactions tend to follow. First, a perpetual
search for the 'right way' to rectify the relationship with this
extremely demanding God, and this may lead to attachment to an
evangelical cult or to one of the several fundamentalist sects now
populating the religious world. A second option is the partial or
complete abandonment of religious adherence: sometimes in total
despair of ever being able to measure up, but more frequently, a
tendency to slide pathetically into a spiritual wasteland – quite a
common move in today's Western world. Thirdly, an internalised
sense of rage and bitterness, overtly aimed at religious systems, and
occasionally at God; what is really hurting here is not the oppressive religious system, but a deep hurt from one's past that continues
to fester under the destructive impact of religious belief. Abandonment of the belief system will not in itself resolve or heal the hurt,
but is likely to offer a temporary respite from the crippling fear.

2. *Escapism.* There is a great deal of truth in Marx's perception that
religion can become an opium of the people. In this case it does not
help them to cope with, resolve or endure the meaninglessness they
experience in life; rather they use religion to rationalise what is happening around them, sometimes to the extent of totally abandoning
all attempts to rectify their problems – God will solve them for us!

The notion of abandonment into God's hands often occurs in
religious culture and in popular religious devotion. Positively, it
invites us to a place of greater equanimity and trust in God and in
life, but for religious devotees it all too easily becomes an excuse to
opt out of real engagement with the challenges of our daily existence. Not unrelated is the tendency in the Western world for
political leaders to shirk moral and ethical responsibility, on the
understanding that these belong to the work of the churches and to
the realm of formal religions.

The escapist attitude is often related to the pervasive role which dualisms play in formal religions. As already indicated, the dualistic world-view, which underpins a great deal of formal religion, inculcates a tendency to escape the perceived evil for the sake of the fantasised good. The challenge of mature spirituality is to learn to engage and live with both.

3. *Moralism*. Religionists claim access to a higher, guiding wisdom in the light of which they claim the right to legislate and dictate what is and what is not morally acceptable. Because of patriarchal and dualistic overtones, a great deal of moralism is aimed at individual behaviour, with little or no cognisance of the surrounding culture and its influences. There are also strong undercurrents of control, not merely over specific behaviour but over people in their entire way of living.

Whereas law is meant to protect and liberate people towards fuller life and a greater sense of responsibility, moralism can inculcate a blind, rigid allegiance, begetting a false sense of self-righteousness leading to moral imperialism. When this imperialism takes on collective power then we have all the ingredients for racial apartheid, economic exploitation or even nuclear warfare, all in the name of the false God of moralism.

4. *Domination and control*. Although every religion claims to be at the service of people in leading them to a more spiritual and enlightened way of life, in practice all religion retains a strong semblance of the patriarchal world out of which religion emanated in the first place. Little wonder, then, that the more recently developed systems pride themselves in being monotheistic and openly pursue a policy of proselytising the 'unconverted'. All religion carries sectarian undercurrents, a widespread belief that 'my system is better than all others'.

5. *Idolatry*. Every shadow experience tends to include dimensions that contradict so blatantly the basic beliefs of life (in a person or a system) that it is inconceivable that they would find a place in one's behaviour. This is precisely the area where the shadow is most deep and difficult to acknowledge. All the religions claim to have right views and understandings of God, and how God impacts upon our world. The more strongly this conviction is held, the more idolatrous it is likely to become.

Many things have been attempted to rehabilitate those disillusioned by religious apathy or bigotry, and in not a few cases the adherents of the religious system have attempted honest and open criticism to improve the quality of what they offer. Such efforts belong to the system itself and tend to be blind to the power and impact of the shadow. The shadow points to a deeper malaise, requiring a much more drastic form of redress, one that reconnects us with more fundamental questions. Spirituality rather than religion furnishes the wisdom and understanding we are pursuing in the exploration of these deeper questions.

Returning to the sacred story

As already intimated, it is the rediscovery and reclaiming of spirituality rather than religion that befits the spiritual search of our time. What is exciting in this undertaking is the fresh and expanded horizons that are opened up. A whole other world, largely subverted by patriarchy, seeks our attention and engages our creative imagination. So much from the inherited past and the prevailing present need to be reviewed and reclaimed in a radically new way.

Beyond the rational, so-called enlightened world of the recent past lie reservoirs of wisdom and vision, which defy linear thought and even spoken language itself. The ability to use verbal speech and communication is quite a recent acquisition for *homo sapiens*, usually dated to 100,000 years ago. That means that for at least 90 per cent of our existence as a human species we communicated and engaged with life using the non-verbal mode. We attribute a type of literalist significance to the spoken and written word that undermines the power of the pre-verbal experience, much of which is still embedded in the collective psyche of humanity. We often assume the pre-verbal stage of our development to be one of savagery, darkness, delusion and ignorance. The pre-verbal being we assume to be more 'animal' than 'human', driven by destructive instinct rather than by the capacity for intelligent action (a view that is comprehensively refuted by Mithen, 1996).

Obviously, I do not wish to exalt our ancient ancestors over and above our contemporaries. I do wish to counter the naïve optimism that assumes humanity in its present state to be a highly developed intelligent life-form, the like of which has never been around before. The long-lost wisdom, it seems to me, is our tendency to ignore, or at least underplay, our identity as an evolutionary, spiritual species. We, humans, belong to an unfolding story of an estimated four million years (Leakey, 1995). Our evolution in turn belongs to a larger story, of the home planet, Earth, and the unfolding universe itself. Our species structure and meaning is not just the product of the past few hundred or thousand years; we carry within our very being, individually and collectively, the dreams and aspirations, the traumas and struggles of millennia, perhaps even of billennia.

Our story is a sacred story, not because of us humans, and the religious systems we have helped to develop. The Originating Mystery (God, or whatever name you wish to use) was at work in creation for billions of years before we ever came to be. Creation itself is a tapestry of incomprehensible elegance, in both its light and shadow, and far outstretches our intellectual and spiritual powers of comprehension. Our surest and most reassuring way to get in touch with the mystery within which we live and grow is by connecting with the sacred story itself. The story itself is our primary wellspring of meaning and purpose.

Much of the story we know nothing about, not because it is inaccessible to us, but because we have basically turned our back on its narration. We have been so preoccupied trying to conquer and control the world – in the past 10,000 years particularly – that we have been unable to listen, to behold, to contemplate and to comprehend the message of the deeper story. Instead of engaging with our world – and our own role within it – we have been trying to master the world. That we should be about mastering the universe is a convoluted perception of our own deranged imaginations, and not a divine command as adherents of the monotheistic religions try to claim.

How we view and understand ourselves, very much depends on how we understand the larger reality or realities to which we belong, and without which our lives are seriously deprived, humanly and spiritually. Our isolationism, our sense of separation which our patriarchal consciousness cherishes so stubbornly, is our greatest anomaly. It pitches us into that alienation and loneliness that breeds so much despair, destruction and spiritual emptiness in our world.

Over the past few decades we, in the West, have begun to reclaim some of the spiritual power of the pre-verbal stage of our development. The hunger for meditation and quietness, in religious or psychotherapeutic circles, but also among ordinary people, is just one reminder, not of regression, but of a desire to connect more deeply. So, too, is the interest in tribal religions, folklore, native rituals. The desire among women in particular for more feminine, inclusive modes of worship has deep archetypal roots that external critics are unable to comprehend or appreciate. Finally, the rediscovery of our cosmos as the unfolding drama of divine co-creativity evokes today profound spiritual sentiments, of a depth and quality outstripping formal religious allegiance. The challenge of the new cosmology, and its profound spiritual implications for our future, is the subject to which we now turn attention.

— 6 —

Spirituality and the creative universe

Unless it receives a new blood transfusion from matter, Christian spirituality may well lose its vigour and become lost in the clouds.

Teilhard de Chardin

Everything that is in the heavens, on the earth, and under the earth is penetrated with connectedness, penetrated with relatedness.

Hildegarde of Bingen

SUSPICION OF 'THE WORLD' and distrust of what goes on there feature significantly in all the great religious traditions. Spiritual fulfilment is perceived to belong to another realm, a life hereafter, a world to come. In that realm beyond, we are told that things endure for ever, sustained by the eternal and permanent reality of God. To desire the fulfilment that belongs to the hereafter is the goal of many spiritual disciplines and the ultimate desire of the spiritual search.

Consequently, the spiritual seeker is encouraged to distance oneself from the domain of 'this world' with its connotations of precariousness, unreliability, transitoriness, a place of sin and temptation. Hence, the advice to flee the world, abandon the world, forsake the world, all to procure the salvation of your soul in the realm beyond, the domain of completion and perfection. Today, Christian spirituality does not tend to advocate this policy overtly, but covertly this approach still exercises a powerful influence and is often invoked with great virulence by evangelical sects and cults.

In many of the great religions one finds echoes of this same dualism, between the all-perfect transcendent God and the immanent, incomplete creature in a creation that is itself essentially flawed and imperfect. Although Christianity alone posits the dogma of original sin, the notion that creation awaits purification and redemption in another realm, nirvana or whatever, permeates a great deal of official religion.

The tendency to attribute sin and imperfection to the natural order is another deviation of our patriarchal past. In the subconscious and conscious attempts to undermine the power of the Great Earth Mother, we also began to de-sacralise the creation itself. In setting ourselves over against the created order we began to perceive it as another adversarial force to be conquered and controlled. Spurred on by our self-deluded God-image – the great conqueror from on high – we sought to undermine and denounce all that we encountered from below.

In what is perhaps the greatest 'Freudian slip' of all time – in the opening chapter of the Hebrew scriptures – we acknowledge that all creation is, and was perceived by God to be, good; then, humans arrive on the scene, and under the influence of male domination, pain, suffering, conflict and barbarity enter the world. The forces of alienation are not introduced by God, but by male humans, who deviously and conveniently blame the woman for the mess that has been caused. The patriarchal will-to-power knows no limits in attempting to satisfy its insatiable desires.

What is the new cosmology?

There are many indications in today's world that this patriarchal compulsion is a spent force, although still prevalent in all our major institutions. Many people have begun to reclaim their freedom and creativity and gradually are shaking off the shackles of political imperialism and religious dogmatism. Despite the fact that many people drift in a spiritual wasteland, a significant proportion have taken the courageous risk of faith to abandon the staid securities of the past and walk the desert road to new spiritual horizons. Foremost among these are the spiritual seekers who are rediscovering our creative cosmos and reconnecting with the innate sacredness of planet Earth itself. This unfolding vision – which I explore at length in another work (Ó Murchú, 1997) – is often referred to as the new cosmology.

In 1948, the astronomer Fred Hoyle wrote: 'Once a photograph of the Earth taken from outside is available . . . a new idea, as powerful as any in history will be let loose.' The photograph was taken in 1969. It depicts our home planet – suspended in space – an image of one Earth, with water and landmass blended together, devoid of the scars of ethnic and national boundaries. The picture has become something of a sacred icon, a poignant reminder of the beauty and fragility of the Earth we inhabit.

As Hoyle had intimated, the photograph evoked a quality of response which is difficult to put into words. The image itself awakens feelings of awe and wonder, a sense of belonging and a sense of mystery. Merely looking at the picture convinces one that there is more to this image than what meets the eye. We are engaging with something we have known for ages and, yet, there it is in front of us as if we were seeing it for the first time.

That, too, was the reaction of many of the astronauts as they began to share their experience of seeing the Earth from outer space, and particularly in the course of the first journey to the moon (cf. pp. 47–49 above). We need to remember that these were people from many different countries, of diverse cultural and religious backgrounds, schooled in rational science which dispassionately views the Earth as dead, inert matter, and lo, we hear them describe planet Earth in poetic, mystical and spiritual language.

The experience of the astronauts – widely shared among those who have journeyed to outer space – is, perhaps, the most convincing evidence we have that planet Earth should be regarded as an alive organism. The notion of our Earth being an organism, rather than an inanimate object, has had a long and fragmented history. It flourished during the Middle Ages but was gradually superseded by the rationalism of classical science – from the sixteenth century until very recent times.

In our own time, the notion of an alive Earth has surfaced again, under the theory of the Gaia hypothesis, developed by James Lovelock and Lynn Margulis. The theory invites us to regard our home planet as a unified, living organism, with an amazing and intricate capacity to grow, develop and regenerate from its own innate resourcefulness. The mainstream scientific community tends to react rather negatively to this idea, although a softening of attitude seems to have taken place in recent years.

The Gaia hypothesis commanded a degree of fascination and engagement throughout the 1970s and 1980s; the more we pursued the idea of an alive Earth, the more we began to intuit that the universe at large is also alive, and functions, too, as a unified, creative organism. This latter conviction lies at the heart of the new cosmology.

Cosmology – the study of the universe and what goes on within it – has aroused human curiosity for thousands of years.

Throughout the era of classical science, we adopted a strategy of observation and verification, trying to figure out how the universe works. We did the observing and checking out; we set the criteria and we made the deductions. All of which led to a view of the universe, not for what it is in itself, but what we decide it could or should be. This tendency, whereby we try to impose our understanding on how things work in the world, is what contemporary writers refer to as anthropocentrism. It is probably the most destructive force at work in the world of our time.

The Australian writer, Paul Collins (1995, p. 18), describes this phenomenon as follows:

Anthropocentrism refers to our focus on the human and the belief that we are the final purpose of the cosmos. It is the unconscious assumption that the Earth exists simply for humankind and that its total meaning and entire value is derived from us. . . . We take ourselves and our needs as the focus, norm and final arbiter of all that exists.[6]

The challenge now facing us, a key element of the new cosmology, is to forgo our insatiable urge to manipulate and control everything to our satisfaction, and instead reassess what it really means to exist within the larger creation, which we experience primarily in our capacity as creatures of planet Earth. To do this, we need to understand afresh – perhaps for the first time – that we inhabit a planet (and a universe) whose existence pre-dates us by billions of years and whose capacity to produce life far outstretches our potential and creativity as human beings. To obtain some sense of this larger picture, it is useful to reflect on the story of evolution itself as it unfolds over the past fifteen to twenty billion years. What I offer here is a poetic resume of that enthralling story.

In the beginning . . .

In the beginning was silence, the eternal stillness of being and becoming, a pregnant restlessness, swelling up within the creative vacuum, exploding forth in a volcano-type irruption of unlimited possibility, known in our time as the Big Bang.

Energy exploded as in a massive fireball, evolving into what we now know to be the dominant forces at work in the universe: gravitation, nuclear strong, nuclear weak and electromagnetism. Before one-millionth of a second had passed, the universe had cooled sufficiently for elementary particles – electrons, neutrons and protons – to form. Three minutes later, as the cooling process continued, neutrons and protons combined to form stable atomic nuclei, initially those of hydrogen and helium. Life was dancing into being with prodigious creativity.

Swimme & Berry (1992) depict with great lucidity the evolving tapestry of the subsequent fifteen billion years, a time-span our limited imaginations can scarcely comprehend, yet one that continues to form and affect the Earth we inhabit and the personal well-being of each one of us. It seems to have taken a few billion years for galactic clouds to break up and pave the way for the evolution of the first stars, which duly exploded into elegant supernovas, giving birth to our own solar system and, in due course, producing the carbon which today is a central element of every living creature, humans included.

In due course there emerged, on a micro-scale, life-forms to match the elegance and grandeur of the larger reality. Cellular life evolved its own creative pattern: first the molecules combined to form cells, which over the millennia manifested a great array of forms ranging from bacteria to algae, plants, corals, worms, insects, clams, starfish, animals and humans.

We, humans, are considered to be the most highly developed life-form currently inhabiting planet Earth (and the entire cosmos, it would seem). What we know about the universe is what we have discovered, and the more we unravel the meaning of life, the more aware we become of how little we do know. Currently, it is estimated that we understand little more than one per cent of the entire evolutionary process. This growing realisation of how little we do know will not diminish our significance in the universe; quite the contrary, it seems to be awakening a new search for meaning, begetting the fascination and exploration known in our time as the new cosmology.

Why a new cosmology?

The 'old cosmology' was based on a set of ideas in people's minds rather than on a set of facts assumed to be the basis of all reality. It was a human invention, based on limited imagination, often validated by questionable religious motifs. It was strongly influenced by the prevailing, masculine consciousness which sought to 'conquer and control' everything in life. Accordingly, we tended to divide our experience into contrasting opposites: spirit versus matter, earth versus heaven, body versus soul, sacred versus secular, dualistic categories which were supposed to explain reality, but in fact are mental notions rather than true descriptions of life.

In the same vein, we perceived the cosmos to be comprised of this world, a materialistic, transitory and illusory existence, and the next world, the realm of completion, durability and eternal fulfilment. To get us from this world to the next became the primary task of the major religions, with their differing but complementary notions of salvation and enlightenment.

The 'old cosmology' is often depicted as originating with the rise of classical science in the sixteenth and seventeenth centuries when we came to regard the universe as a great machine and understood it to operate primarily in a mechanistic way. But, as already noted, it goes back much further than that, right back to about 8000 BCE when patriarchy was born from within the womb of the Agricultural Revolution.

The patriarchal, mechanistic view of the universe no longer resonates with our contemporary experience as a human, planetary and spiritual species, nor does it resonate with the changing spiritual and theological aspirations of our time. It has brought significant benefits to humankind, but at the price of enormous pain, suffering and destruction. Describing its negative impact, Thomas Berry (1988, pp. 134–35) writes:

> During this time the human mind lived in the narrowest bonds it has ever experienced. The vast mythic, visionary, symbolic world with its all-pervasive numinous qualities was lost. Because of this loss humanity made its terrifying assault upon the Earth with an irrationality that is stunning in enormity while we were being assured that this is the way to a better, more humane, more reasonable world.

This mechanised and functional view of the world (and of the Earth particularly) is now in irreversible decline and in a state of progressive disintegration. With its demise we find ourselves challenged and called to engage with a new sense of what our world is about, and that we call the new cosmology.

Main features of the new cosmology

We describe two dominant world-views as old and new. As we continue to expore the story and evolution of our universe, and reclaim the more ancient spiritual traditions of our peoples, we realise that this distinction is irrelevant and also needs to be discarded. In engaging with the new cosmology, we realise that life universally thrives on forces that have existed from time immemorial, but which we are now understanding in a new way. Because the patriarchal and mechanistic approaches of the past few thousand years undermined our larger vision, we are now invited to retrieve what has been lost or subverted during that time.

1. *Story*. Today, science claims to be the primary body of knowledge with the aid of which we can understand what happens in our world. And science emphasises the importance of facts and figures that are observed, tested and verified in ways that make sense to human reason, which scientists consider to be the supreme form of wisdom.

Many people, however, from various fields of learning, realise that science on its own cannot fully comprehend or understand our world and how it functions. Moreover, the unfolding spiritual consciousness of our time remains unconvinced that rational, factual information, on its own, can lead to the discovery of meaningful truth. The intuitive wisdom of our age veers towards a multidisciplinary approach. We need the wisdom and insight, not of one, but of several branches of learning. And more important still, we need to be open to the innate wisdom of the universe itself in its creative, evolutionary unfolding, often following a set of laws which we do not fully understand.

Consequently, we adopt the notion of story as the best possible means to comprehend what the universe is about. The universe itself is forever telling its own story, manifesting its prodigious fertility in the bursting forth of life that we see all around us. With our human consciousness and intelligence, we can name many of its creative elements and deepen our understanding of those processes. But unless we do so within the context of the evolving story itself, our namings frequently will fall short of the larger truth, and thus may distort the creative and spiritual intent of evolution itself.

Referring to the significance of the universe's unfolding story, Brian Swimme has written:

The new cosmic story, emerging into human awareness, over-whelms all previous conceptions of the universe, for the simple reason that it draws them all into its comprehensive fullness. Who can learn what this means and remain calm?

In fact, we can remain calm because the story does not overwhelm us. We are an integral dimension of that story. In narrating the story of creation we are telling our own story, at a very real, personal level. As we weave the story and are woven by it, fresh hope and meaning awaken in our hearts; we are drawn into the contemplative awareness of being participants (and not mere observers) in what Swimme & Berry describe as 'the narrative of cosmogenesis'.

Cosmogenesis describes the working of the universe as one in a continuous state of becoming, begetting fresh life and possibility, ever changing and, thus, ever new. We can never fully comprehend what it is about, and we don't need to, because an intelligent universe is capable of dealing with its own unfolding in an intelligent way, and all its constituent parts, including us, humans, provided that those parts co-operate in a benign and interdependent fashion.

2. *Alive*. We have already referred to the emerging understanding of planet Earth as an alive organism and the research underpinning that notion, popularly known as the Gaia hypothesis. The suggestion that our universe is also alive is much more compelling at an intuitive, spiritual and evolutionary level, but a great deal more difficult to substantiate to the satisfaction of the mainstream scientific community.

Swimme & Berry (1992, pp. 17, 19) describe the innate creativity of the universe in these words:

Originating power brought forth a universe. . . . The universe as it expands itself and establishes its basic coherence, reveals the elegance of activity, necessary to hold open all the immensely complex possibilities of its future blossoming.

This is not a conclusion reached merely on the basis of rigorous scientific research, nor on profound religious insight, but primarily on their experience of the ten-year project which culminated in their classic work, *The Universe Story*. In a contemplative ambience of listening and dialogue, alone and with many others, Swimme &

Berry set out to write a book in which they would facilitate the universe in telling its own story with a minimum of interference or interpretation from human beings. This may well be the first of a new generation of spiritual classics, seeking to outgrow the corrupting influence of anthropocentric religiosity.

The reader is left with an indelible impression of the universe's amazing resilience in the face of overwhelming odds pointing to chaos and annihilation. Time and again, the universe seems to draw on innate resources to launch itself into a new phase of growth, development and transformation. We need not invoke an external divine agent to explain this growth, because the universe's own propensity to self-organise, to self-renew and take qualitative leaps forward, is all too apparent. Indeed, if divine intervention is at work, then it is primarily coming from within the universe and not from outside it.

In what sense is the universe alive? For those who can tune in to the power of the evolutionary narrative, this question is both superfluous and unnecessary. It is like asking why does a story (e.g. a fairy tale) grip a child's imagination? Because story touches the deepest layers of the human psyche, it awakens the imagination and transforms our understanding in a way that cerebral (heady), rational information can never hope to achieve.

The mystery is not in how we understand what it means to be 'alive' but in the power of the story to awaken that sense of being alive in the depth of our own being, and project us into a new way of relating with the life-force that enlivens the universe, along with everything in it, including ourselves. Life in its true meaning cannot be fully understood or celebrated apart from the big picture of universal life, from within which everything takes ultimate meaning and purpose. As the astronauts detected intuitively and expressed so poetically, life takes on a whole new meaning of depth, beauty and meaning when we engage with it on the larger scale. As living beings we are all but suffocated from cultural, religious and scientific minimalism. Our passion for rigorous, minute detail is choking us to death.

3. *Interdependence.* In fact an important key to unlocking the meaning of life in our universe is to try to understand the interdependent, interconnected way in which all reality is interlinked. Everything in the universe needs everything else. Eliminate

any one layer, or dimension; destroy any one life-form, and all others are threatened with extinction.

Independence is so deeply ingrained in our Western self-understanding – and validated by our formal religious systems – that we find it difficult to engage with the notion of interdependence. Many fear that it might erode individual uniqueness and personal identity. Long after we have accepted interdependence as a central notion, we may continue to behave in ways that clearly are not interdependent. The Western mind-set and the enculturation accompanying it strike very deep roots in our personal and social psyche.

Swimme & Berry (1992, pp. 71–78) offer a reassuring way of dealing with this challenge. They describe the universe's own creative process in terms of differentiation, interiority and communion. Differentiation refers to the fact that everything in creation is totally unique; according to the Christian scriptures, every hair on the human head is numbered (unique), so is every subatomic particle in the universe. Individual uniqueness is characteristic of every aspect of life on the large and small scale alike.

Interiority refers to the innate potential of every organism to grow, develop and become, to blossom into its full potential. When we engage with the universe as an organism, then everything is deemed to be alive. Consequently, even those things which to the human eye seem inert and lifeless, e.g., a stone, are endowed with an interior will-to-life within which their fuller potential begins to unfold.

4. *Communion.* However, the interior process of self-becoming (autopoiesis) which contributes to individual uniqueness, is not geared to ego-inflation or to self-aggrandizement, but to the coming together of all things in mutual interdependence. Because we live in a universe of curved space-time, everything is destined to encounter everything else. In fact, we belong to a universe in which belonging is a primary touchstone for the growth and development of all life-forms. (This is the basis of our capacity to relate, which we'll explore at length in Chapter 7.)

Without this mutual interdependence, nothing attains its full potential. It is in the context of communion, and not through competitive, robust individualism, that all life-forms discover their true identity and attain the realisation of their full potential.

5. *Paradox.* Paradox is not something we talk about in our daily lives. Yet, it is a central element of our human experience, one which often surfaces in our spiritual and religious traditions. In religious terms, paradox refers to those puzzling events or statements which on the surface seem to be contradictions, but in fact embody a deeper meaning. Examples from the Christian scriptures include: the magnificence of God manifested to our world in the form of a vulnerable infant; statements such as: 'The first shall be last and the last first' (Mk 10:31), or the words of St Paul: 'When I am weak, then I am strong' (2 Cor. 12:10).

From a Christian viewpoint, perhaps, the greatest contradiction of all is the fact that Jesus had to die such a cruel, ignominious death before being able to experience resurrection. Jesus offers no explanation for this baffling paradox. This example is particularly relevant to our time since that same process of death (destruction) and resurrection (fresh creation) recurs many times in the evolutionary story of our universe.

In the past, some scientists and theologians gave scant attention to the notion of evolution, arguing that it was impossible to trace the evolutionary development of the universe in a rational, sequential manner and, therefore, we couldn't take evolution seriously. They often point to those massive gaps in the evolutionary process (sometimes covering millions of years) when, apparently, nothing was happening (detailed by Verschuur, 1978; also Leakey, 1992, pp. 354ff.; Leakey & Lewin, 1996). These lapses often follow massive, disruptive extinctions (as in the Triassic era 210 million years ago, lasting an estimated 100 million years, or the Cretacian extinction around 65 million years ago, lasting some 20 million years).

As we listen afresh to the evolutionary story, we are rediscovering that destruction and fresh creation are essential to each other as complementary dimensions of the universe's paradoxical nature.

In fact, our universe thrives on paradox, those apparent contradictions through which we glimpse some of life's most elegant, mysterious and beautiful breakthroughs. The process of respiration (i.e. the ability to breathe) is nature's response to the cataclysmic destruction which oxygen originally caused in one of nature's best-known paradoxes. Others include the process of heterotrophy whereby creatures eat each other to survive and grow, or the cycle of birth–death–rebirth so prevalent in the natural world.

6. *Revelation.* The notion of revealed truth features in all the world religions. Christianity has always claimed unique access to divine revelation over and above that available through other faiths, a superior claim based on the understanding that the coming of Christ on Earth supersedes God's self-disclosure to other religions.

This conviction, highly cherished by many theologians, and vehemently safeguarded by many churches, carries far less weight and meaning for the rank-and-file of Christianity. Increasing numbers of Christians perceive it to be a form of Christian imperialism that begets sectarian exclusiveness and oppressive religious dogmatism.

The new cosmology offers a radically different understanding. It claims that creation itself is the primary revelation; that God's life and love become visible and tangible first and foremost in the unfolding of universal life. In all its aspects, including the polarities of light and shadow, creation and destruction, the divine becomes manifest; creation glows with the light and life of God. In this context, each of the religions is deemed to be a particular crystallisation of God's revelation for a specific time and culture. All of which suggests that the mainstream religions are destined to last for limited periods of time, and have a cultural significance for specific peoples rather than a relevance for the whole of humanity.

Spirituality rather than religion is the central concern of the new cosmology. It seeks to explore the spiritual meaning of the evolutionary process over the billions of years before humanity ever came to be. Within the time-span of human evolution, it wishes to explore our spiritual inheritance covering some 70,000 years of human existence, long before formal religions evolved. And, finally, it calls special attention to that fascinating epoch in Paleolithic times (c. 40000–10000 BCE) when we humans, across the inhabited Earth of the time, worshipped God as woman, the Great Earth Mother Goddess.

The new cosmology is not seeking to overthrow formal religion with its claim of having special access to divine revelation. Instead, it seeks to re-locate God's co-creativity where it perceives it to belong primarily: within the co-creative process at large, and not merely within the minute time-span of the past few thousand years, during which the formal religions evolved.

In positing this fresh and challenging view of revelation, the new cosmology affirms a central conviction of the present work, namely, that the spiritual unfolding of life – at every level – is governed by a grandeur and elegance which we humans seek to control to our own detriment and usually to the detriment of creation also. This is a wisdom which, fortunately, is out of our control. The supreme spiritual task of our time is to let go of our anthropocentric craving for dominance and superiority and learn to live interdependently with our co-creative God.

7. *Belonging*. Throughout the Agricultural Era (since about 8000 BCE) we regarded the Earth (and the universe) as an object to be conquered and controlled. We set ourselves up as the masters of creation, which we ruthlessly manipulated and exploited for our own self-inflated prosperity. We set ourselves over against creation and sought to justify that adversarial stance with the self-deluded conviction that God, religion and the church are also fundamentally opposed to creation.

At the heart of the new cosmology is the conviction that we belong to the universe, not the universe to us. To quote Thomas Berry (1988, p. 195):

> We cannot discover ourselves without first discovering the universe, the Earth, and the imperatives of our own being. Each of these has a creative power and a vision far beyond any rational thought or cultural creation of which we are capable. Nor should we think of these as isolated from our own individual being or from the human community. We have no existence except within the Earth and within the universe.

We are one life-form, an integral dimension, of a co-creative universe in which every aspect is unique, but also interdependent. No one group has the right to lord it over the others, but the very attempt to do so will alienate that group from the cosmic family within which we all find our true identity.

Our participation in the communion of all life-forms does not dissolve our uniqueness into some type of an amorphous cosmic conglomerate. Quite the contrary, it is from within this creative interdependence that we discover initially, and rediscover many times, our unique identity as individual people and as a human species. Not alone is our sense of cosmic belonging a safeguard against alienation and anomie; it also provides the ambience for our growth and unfolding as human creatures, individually and collectively.

When we go it alone and seek to claim and impose an inflated superior role, in the name of mastery or some other patriarchal motif, it is then that we are in danger of behaving like parasites who reap havoc on the womb that nourishes and sustains us, and eventually succumb to self-destructive behaviour, often culminating in inevitable self-annihilation.

Today, we humans, with our several human caricatures, are perched on the threshold of massive self-destruction. Some theorists feel that it is already too late to save ourselves from the irredeemable mess we have created in the world. Our will-to-power has become compulsive, addictive and highly destructive. It will take something verging on a global miracle to save us from ourselves; ironically, that miracle may require the elimination of *homo sapiens*!

The new cosmology, and its accompanying spirituality, requires us to treat extinction (especially of our own species) with the utmost seriousness. Even if we can't bring about the desired change of heart to save our own species, we owe it to the rest of creation to diminish the destructive behaviour which currently creates so much pain and suffering for other life-forms.

We also need to face the grim reality of extinction in the reassuring hope that when all our efforts fail, the universe itself can rescue the will-to-life in a way that we humans can never do. Whether or not the universe considers us a seemly species worth saving is, perhaps, the most urgent dilemma facing us, requiring profound contemplative discernment.

8. *Consciousness.* Our understanding of how life unfolds in the universe is heavily influenced by the classical modelling of Newtonian science and Cartesian philosophy. In this approach, everything is considered to be a machine and its true essence is determined by its external, visible and tangible contours. Only the physical, material dimension is considered to be real.

Although Christian theology claims to be based on divinely revealed truth, it, too, has been heavily influenced by classical thought-patterns: hence, its hermeneutic of logical, rational argument, seeking to establish theological fact on the grounds of pure reason. The practice of religion tends to follow a similar cerebral approach: proclaiming the message of faith, but often seeking to ground it in humanly designed structures which frequently over-shadow and even undermine the spiritual vision.

Today, both science and theology are invited to consider that the really real is based more on consciousness than on rationally observed fact or structure. The quantum theory in physics has opened up something of the creative potential inherent in those processes of nature which human senses on their own are incapable of comprehending. On the cosmological level, we are rediscovering the power inherent in the creative vacuum which potentiates the 'fields', which in turn materialise in a whole set of activities and structures which we can observe, and participate in, in our daily lives.

Danah Zohar (1993, pp. 141–42) is one of several contemporary scientists exploring a deeper understanding of consciousness which she describes as an active agent within the process of evolution, constantly forming new, ordered, coherent wholes, new patterns that draw chaos into order, or that draw simpler patterns into more complex ones:

> It would be like a whirlpool drawing surrounding water molecules into itself, only in the case of consciousness the 'molecules' being drawn in actually would be fragments of experience, or bits of information. On a quantum interpretation, the evolution of consciousness, like the evolution of the universe, proceeds from variation, to selection, to further variation.

The consciousness we possess as human beings, contrary to being a special endowment with which we seek to lord it over the rest of creation, needs to be freshly understood as an integral dimension of the 'intelligence' that permeates all life in the universe. The greater intelligence is the superior form, not ours. We belong to a reality greater than ourselves, an envelope of consciousness informing our awareness, intuition and imagination – in what is essentially an intelligent universe. All our thoughts, dreams and aspirations arise from this cosmic wellspring within which we live and grow, and are empowered to realise our full potential as planetary, cosmic crea-tures. Anything short of this global engagement leaves us unfulfilled, frustrated and ultimately alienated from God and humanity.

The fear of letting go

Some consider the new cosmology to be a pantheistic fantasy-world in which the uniqueness of both God and the human is compromised. There is a great fear that individuality might be undermined or eroded; that God becomes so cosmic as to be effectively impersonal. Perhaps the central concern here is our understanding of personality, and the tendency in former times to reduce all notions of personhood to the masculine, self-sufficient achiever of the prevailing patriarchal culture.

As outlined above, the new cosmology thrives on relatedness and interdependence. These qualities also apply to the divine life-force which impregnates and sustains the created order, a God we perceive to be primarily a being-for-relatedness. This offers fresh insight into the Christian notion of God as Trinity – a concept that has parallels in many of the great religions and in the ancient forms of Goddess worship. (For further elucidation, see Abraham, 1994; McLean, 1989.)

Far from being an agnostic or pantheistic development, the new cosmology evokes deep sentiments of love, respect, tenderness, care and creativity. It expands the narrow horizons of both traditional science and orthodox religion, and forges fresh connections with the long-lost feminine and intuitive values of our spiritual heritage. It invites us to outgrow the dualistic opposition of the sacred and the secular, the earthly and the spiritual, challenging us to engage with the God who transcends all our human distinctions and yet enters profoundly into our creative reality as human, planetary and cosmic creatures.

As indicated many times thus far, this renewed spiritual vision invokes new ways of relating at every level of life. The capacity to relate is itself a central dimension of all spiritual experience. It is that key feminine value that underpins another major strand of contemporary spirituality: the rediscovery of the feminine, the topic to which we now turn our attention.

Reclaiming the feminine heart

We in the West are haunted by the loss of our Mother.

Caitlin Matthews

We call people 'mad' when they see things from a perspective different from
our own. Since we do not gladly entertain the notion that we are wrong, we
are more than ready to denounce such people as crazy, mad fools. . . . But
what if the ones we call 'mad' are really sane?

Robert McAfee Brown

F EMINISM IS THE NAME WE GIVE to one of the most creative
and volatile movements of our time. It is often depicted as a militant reaction of disgruntled women who seek to overthrow all
semblance of male power and domination, a defensive caricature
adopted by the dominant male culture that justifiably feels threatened
by this powerful upsurge. Adopting a defensive role, however, has little spiritual, cultural or human meaning either for the protagonists or
those on the defensive. The real meaning is located at a much deeper
level which we will seek to uncover in the present chapter.

The power of the feminine in human history is best assessed by
connecting with our ancient cultural story in pre-patriarchal times.
I do not wish to suggest that a superior, matriarchal culture preceded the current patriarchal one; that is a contention that need not
concern us now. My interest is in the prevalent culture of the
Paleolithic era, dated from c. 40000 BCE to c. 10000 BCE. Although
that too is a specific and limited time-span of our unfolding as a
human species, it is one about which we know a great deal that our
patriarchal world-view has attempted to erode, and fortunately not
with total success.

The sins of patriarchy

Nearly all feminists claim that we have inherited a false ordering of
reality, characterised by three dominant features: patriarchy,

androcentrism and sexism. These are three different, but inter-related, aspects of the oppression felt by women particularly, but also undermining a more meaningful relationship with our planet Earth and with all life-forms within it.

Patriarchy, as defined elsewhere in this book, refers to those masculine orientations of possession and control, setting the authoritarian male over against everything in life (nature included), which is understood to be there for the conquering.

Androcentrism refers to a one-sided approach to all relationships – whether human or earthly – whereby the male is projected as the stronger, the better, the holier, the more authentic.

Sexism has been defined as an exclusive ordering of life by way of gender. Whilst biological sex is given, gender is socially and culturally constructed to the advantage of the 'stronger' sex.

Mary Daly (1978, pp. 30–31) offers a more penetrating critique of patriarchy's destructive impact – through what she calls the Eight Deadly Sins of the Fathers:

- *Processions*: we adopt procedures in which we seek to involve people in the unfolding process, but this procedure is often imposed from on high, deceptively giving the impression of a new creative ordering, whereas it is merely another rendition of manipulation and oppression.
- *Professions*: mystifying knowledge and expertise leading to the creation of specialisations (and specialists) for the benefit of those who lord it over others.
- *Possession*: because masculine, dominant power wants to claim control over everything, and dictate how we exercise all our gifts, particularly our creative ones, attributions such as 'demonic possession' consign much creative richness, and especially women's gifts and experiences, to virtual oblivion.
- *Aggression*: destructive violence, perpetuated by men particularly, and often aimed, directly or indirectly, at women and at the environment.
- *Obsession*: male lust with its many projections treating women as sexual objects.
- *Assimilation*: cultural gluttony, whereby living experience is 'eaten up' and consigned to life-inhibiting structures: 'The tyranny of methodolatry hinders new discoveries' (Daly, 1985, p. 11).

- *Elimination*: the ruthless envy or jealousy that makes the other, male or female, feel as if they did not exist.
- *Fragmentation*: the cultural sloth that ensues when we pursue the policy of 'divide and conquer', undermining human initiative and inculcating widespread apathy and anomie.

Daly claims that naming is a primary gift which feminists can offer to our civilisation. She is seeking to confront and transform the patriarchal tendency to label rather than to name. The former refers to those definitions of reality with which we can categorise and denounce what hinders our masculine compulsion towards total control, examples being: schizophrenic, atheist, homosexual, witch, barbarian, etc. Naming, on the other hand, tends to be more open, imaginative and descriptive. In the Christian scriptures, God's name is invoked as a source that empowers people towards action (mission); we name children in Christian baptism to confer on them an identity for the sake of human and creative interaction. Naming is a liberating process.

In terms of spirituality, feminism more than any other contemporary movement, throws open doors that have been not merely closed, but tightly bolted – and not just for centuries, but for millennia. Its re-naming (and in some cases, naming for the first time) is highly creative, provocative, subversive, primordial and archetypal. A whole new world, for long subverted within the enclaves of staid and stultifying religiosity, and aborted by the 'sins of the Fathers' outlined above, is now claiming our attention and allegiance.

A new Reformation?

From within the world of feminist theology and spirituality two approaches are adopted:

1. *Reformist*. The traditions we have adopted, e.g. in the mainstream religions, are couched in language, concepts and rituals which need to be re-thought, reformulated and activated afresh to uncover the deeper, more inclusive meanings that have been subverted. This involves a great deal more than a process of demythologisation or remythologisation. The original cultural context needs to be retrieved and explored in the light of the prevailing patriarchal value-system. In order to retrieve a more holistic vision,

and reconstruct a more inclusive praxis, researchers often have to adopt multi-disciplinary and intuitive tools of investigation. In itself, this approach is original, and in many cases unknown, and thus frequently invites suspicion and disregard from those who claim to possess 'the fullness of truth'.

Many of the better-known Christian feminists adopt this approach: Elizabeth Schussler Fiorenza (1983) in biblical studies; Rosemary Radford Reuther, Carol Christ, Judith Plaskow, Mercy Amba Oduyoye, Chung Hyung Kyung and many others in systematic theology (see the comprehensive overview in King, 1989; Ross & Hilkert, 1995); Rebecca Chopp (1989) and Mary McClintock-Fulkerson (1994) in the study of religious language; Sandra Schneiders (1991), Katherine Zappone (1991) and Maria Harris (1991) in spirituality. They seek to shake the foundations from within, believing that the tradition can be transformed to release the life-blood that lies congealed beneath centuries of congested intellectualism and spiritual impoverishment.

2. *Radical.* The systems we have inherited are so corrupted and depraved by the domination and exploitation of patriarchy that they are effectively beyond redemption, and therefore need to be abandoned and disowned totally. Having shed the depraved baggage of the past, women (and men who identify closely with the feminist consciousness) need to return to and reclaim afresh, their own experience; from within the narration of their own sacred story, past and present, they 're-member' in a way that will generate a new story for a new future. Mary Daly (1973, 1978), Naomi Goldenberg (1979) and Daphne Hampson (1990) are among the better-known advocates of this position.

Even among feminists, the radical position is considered to be an extreme one although no longer set in adversarial opposition to the reformist view, as tended to happen in the 1970s. As Ross and Hilkert (1995, pp. 328–29) point out, the feminist discourse has raised so many complex and engaging questions that it can no longer be reduced to any one or a few key perspectives (also, King, 1994). Indeed, feminism stands unique for its holistic, non-dualistic vision with a comprehensive view of history and culture that stretches the heart and imagination far beyond the mental constructs and cultural paradigms of the predominantly patriarchal modelling of the past 10,000 years.

The radical position is frequently accused of discarding and undermining genuine tradition without which we are rootless and bootless, the victims of every whim and fancy that chance throws up. All of which begs the question – so central to contemporary spirituality – what tradition are we referring to? Feminists of the radical stance have no difficulty with the vision and challenge of the pre-patriarchal era and the profound world-view of Paleolithic times; it has no difficulty with the notion of a co-creative God who transcends the monotheistic religions by millions of years of divinely inspired evolution. In adopting the large-scale vision, feminism poses profoundly challenging and disturbing questions for the understanding of spirituality espoused by the formal religions.

Orthodox spiritualities, of all the religious traditions, suffer from extreme asphyxiation. Within the religious systems, the breadth and depth of God's creativity (the Spirit who breathes where s(he) wills) has been virtually choked by well-intentioned but largely misguided idolatrous gurus. But perhaps, that is what our creative God wishes to happen! Only by the destruction and death of formal religion can we hope to reclaim spirituality where it truly belongs, where it has flourished for billions of years before patriarchal times, in the heart of creation itself. Rescuing spirituality from the shackles of religion would seem to be among the perennial spiritual challenges of our time.

Reclaiming experience seems to be a crucial dynamic as we seek to delineate the key elements of the new spiritual agenda. When feminists use the word 'experience' (see Carr, 1988; Plaskow & Christ, 1989) they employ a breadth and depth that critics frequently fail to comprehend. Our patriarchal culture tends to interpret experience as a fleeting, here-and-now, feeling-based reaction devoid of rational thought, conceptual clarity or historical context. The critique is often based on a mental construct of what we think the feminists are on to, rather than a dialogical engagement with what they are really articulating.

As indicated previously, the feminist vision is deeply connected with myth, history, story and culture to a degree and extent that the rational, conceptual mind of 'the Enlightenment' seems unable to comprehend. When feminists talk about experience it is personal, interpersonal, trans-patriarchal and planetary, all at once. Feminists feel no need to differentiate and fragment their experience; its power rests in its wholism, in the power of the story, and not the facts, that underpin its reality.

As we enter into that deep story, we begin to sense 'movements of the Spirit' which become important pointers in the rediscovery of an authentic spirituality for our time. Feminists offer various namings for those 'movements', but there is broad agreement on the following key elements: relationship, passion, imagination, resistance and solidarity. In fact, these might well be described as the archetypal (foundational) qualities of every genuine spirituality, generating the hope and meaning which people seek in every age.

The capacity to relate

Patriarchy propounds a hierarchical construct for organising and structuring all of reality. Everything is presumed to operate in such a way that there are those who are wiser, holier and better than all others. Relationships are assumed to function from top-down; people are expected to 'know their place and keep it', a guideline which is frequently applied to those at the bottom of the pile but rarely to those at the top.

Much emphasis rests on difference and separation, isolation and exclusion. Everything is analysed (by the head) and understood to exist and operate autonomously. Uniqueness is perceived to be rooted in individual identity. And often that identity is gleaned from dualistic categorisations whereby things (including people) are understood in terms of what they are opposed to. As indicated previously, all dualisms are contructs of the human mind, and not facts of reality. In the process of outgrowing dualistic thought and perception we begin to glean that in the world around us complementary values of both-and are more basic to reality than the dualistic division of either/or.

Feminists are at the cutting edge in renaming the essential nature of life as one of relatedness. Everything is interconnected and interdependent; everything needs everything else to realise its full potential. More importantly, when we look at nature, we quickly realise that things do not receive their identity from some process of isolated, individualistic development, but from the context of relationships. All life-forms owe their origin to the carbon expelled from stars, themselves undergoing annihilation which many scientists today would describe as a process of transformation, and not extinction. Biological procreation in all species requires co-operative interaction based on instinct and attraction. In our interdependent universe, as we saw in Chapter 5, survival and growth are dependent on altruistic, relational behaviour.

The relational mode of being requires a very different set of paradigms from the hierarchical one. The former is more egalitarian, participative and communal in its essential nature. It thrives on a radical form of equality whereby every aspect of life is considered unique irrespective of its place on a hierarchical ladder. Relationships within the interdependent system, in order to function effectively, require openness, trust and freedom. There is no primordial blueprint, or divinely ordained order, whereby things must operate. The meaning and purpose of relationships is determined by the relational interaction itself, and this can vary significantly from one culture or context to the other.

To the patriarchal mind-set this is a prescription for anarchy and chaos. In fact, this is the way things have been in human history for at least four million years; that fact in itself requires profound contemplative attention. If we believe that all history is sacred history (as I do), and we believe that God was at work in creation and in people throughout all that time, then we need to listen to our evolutionary story, particularly to its creative and unstructured unfolding. I am not suggesting that it was totally without structure – as social creatures we always need a structure – but the evidence of the Paleolithic era, the epoch of the Great Mother Goddess, manifests a creative structure which, in comparative terms, seems to have been far more sophisticated and life-giving than the patriarchal structures which dominate our world today. As already indicated, the relational mode was uppermost in the consciousness of Paleolithic peoples.

I also wish to suggest that the major religions bear primary evidence to relatedness as an archetypal dimension of all reality, including our images of the Godhead itself. Consequently, we see in every major religion, with the notable exception of Islam, a trinitarian structure; nature is also richly endowed with the triune configuration (see Greenstein, 1988). The doctrine of the Trinity in Christian theology, from an archetypal viewpoint, transcends the logistical quagmire of trying to contain three 'persons' in One, and highlights the human desire to explore and explain the meaning of Godhead as a relational phenomenon. Whatever else we humans sense about God, deep in our spiritual collective psyche, we believe God to be about relationships.

As we know from human experience and planetary engagement, relationships can never be fully explained or comprehended. In their writings, Carter Heyward (1989), Mary Hunt (1982), John Welwood (1991) and Thomas Moore (1992, 1994) describe vividly the prevailing sense of mystery that gives all relationships vibrancy and depth. It is this unmeasurable quality, which defies all structure, that awakens in the human heart the desire to bond and inter-relate. It is something of the same mysterious force that binds together elements in nature, e.g. the quarks, pointing to the relational nexus of all reality.

Reclaiming the relational mode as the primary dynamic of life, at every level of existence, is probably the single most profound and most provocative claim of feminist spirituality. On this all other understandings – imaginal, conceptual, philosophical and theological – hinge. The relationship is the heart of reality, the core interaction and value around which everything and everybody revolves. From it springs the energy and dynamism to engage creatively and with purpose. And from this comes the conviction and resolve that we cannot go on living with the disordered amd disordering relationships which dominate our world today. The call to work unceasingly for right relationships itself begets another powerful quality of feminist consciousness: passion, a topic we will now explore at some length.

Beyond our *apatheia*

In the Christian spiritual tradition, the Greek term '*apatheia*' has a double significance: in the case of God, it signifies the absence of passions, hence denoting the state of impassibility; in the case of humans, mastery over the passions. The original usage is often linked to the Stoic view of life which considered the passions to be diseases of the soul that are unnatural and intrinsically evil. Consequently, there developed the spiritual ideal of totally eliminating the passions and the desires they produce. The other dominant view seeks to redirect the energy of passion to obtain spiritual freedom, not the suppression of desire, but its purification as envisaged by John Cassian in his concept of purity of heart.

Despite various attempts throughout Christian history to

rehabilitate the emotions and feelings, Christian spirituality has tended towards the more cerebral, rational and analytical mode. We notice it in the tradition of discursive prayer, which interestingly flourished since the seventeenth century, paralleling the cultural developments of classical science, rational thought and machine-based technology. In the discursive method, the initiate is taught to follow a very structured method, using the senses and conscious mind right through. Mental distractions (often arising from feelings and emotions) were considered a hindrance, and if entertained, a sin. The person at prayer was challenged to become an empty receptacle into which God would pour grace and spiritual life. Little wonder that many people became riddled with scruples and that spirituality began to breed neurosis and anxiety rather than purpose and meaning.

This model of the spiritual life is another product of that patriarchal culture which seeks to domesticate and control. I believe that its impact on many women (and some men) has been quite destructive. In seeking to eliminate the passionate aspects of life (pride, creativity, ecstasy, freedom to flow with experience), it has undermined those very qualities which form the essential nature of womanhood. It was a spirituality designed by men, for men and, ironically, practised more rigorously by women, which one can fairly safely suggest was the subconscious, if not conscious, intention of those who designed the package in the first place. The ideal holy person should not be passionately involved in life; (s)he should assume a sense of aloofness (humility), dismissing the concerns of the world as illusive and transitory. Because women are essentially creatures of feeling and innately passionate, they were considered to be sources of temptation for men; consequently, women were to be shunned and avoided by those seriously committed to the spiritual life.

Even a cursory glance at the Christian Gospels, depicting an intensely energetic and enthusiastic Jesus on fire with a new dream, leaves one in little doubt that pathos and not apatheia is a central characteristic of the Christian vision. In fact all the formal religions underestimate this primordial spiritual energy which is innate and essential to the unfolding of human growth. The graphics and statuettes of the great Ice Age exuberate with a wild, uncontrollable exhilaration. Not surprisingly, therefore – for centuries even prior to the Ice Age – dance was the primary mode and language of spirituality.

Feminism, therefore, in seeking the retrieval of passion, is unconsciously empowering us all to reclaim a central dimension of our evolutionary and spiritual story. Whether male or female, we are all endowed with 'fire in the belly', an inner drive towards depth and intensity which manifests in the beauty of poetry, the eroticism of sensuality, the creativity of sexuality, the wild spirit of playfulness, the righteous anger that drives us to work for justice; the divine rage that seeks to eliminate all forms of oppression. Without these intense feelings, and the commitments that they evoke, life would have ceased to exist billions of years ago.

Modern cosmology highlights similar movements within the evolutionary, creative process itself. In the Christian tradition, we find reference to the 'groaning of creation', the birthpangs of new life, the painful defence to protect life against adversarial attack (especially by humans), and the many unexplained evolutionary leaps to great heights of prodigious creativity, manifested now in the millions of species and variegated life-forms that populate our world.

Humanity today, devoid of passionate engagement, is starving the psyche (and spirit) to death. In the Western world, we have become so preoccupied with hedonistic escapism, and self-protective apathy, that all our passion has become narcissistic and largely self-destructive; in the two-thirds world, people suffer grotesquely from the 'crucifixion of passion', caused in large measure by our cumulative projections from the West. In a world devoid of real passion, we become so numbed that we can't see either our own apathetic convolutions of narcissistic empire-building, nor can we, in any real way, feel the cruel pain and suffering we impose upon the vulnerable of our Earth and upon the tortured Earth itself.

The retrieval of passion is one of the most urgent spiritual and cultural requirements of our time. It is only those who feel the depths of pain and joy that can awaken the enthusiasm and motivation to jolt us out of our cultural lethargy. It is that same passionate commitment that will enable the prophets among us to endure the rejection and opposition of patriarchal domination which will continue to subvert and eliminate the visionary whenever and wherever possible. And finally, it is the visionaries of passion, and not the prophets of doom, who can awaken the power of imagination with which we can dream dreams for a better tomorrow.

Set free the imagination

In the West, we are overwhelmed with linear logic and, to a corresponding degree, denuded of creative imagination. Consequently, we expend enormous quantities of energy, effort and money implementing policies and strategies which are so unimaginatively functional and utilitarian that they often leave untouched the yearnings and aspirations of the human heart. Walter Brueggemann (1978, p. 45) states the problem in glaringly simple terms: 'Our culture is competent to implement almost anything and to imagine almost nothing.' Elsewhere Brueggemann (1986, p. 26) writes:

> Resistance, I submit, comes from a frightened, crushed imagination that has been robbed of power precisely because of fear. Indeed, one can note the abysmal lack of imagination in the formation of policy about either international security or domestic economics. We can think of nothing to do except to do more of the same, which generates only more problems and more fear. When we are frightened we want certitude, not porousness.

For so long the voices of women and the wisdom of the feminine have been hiding in the oblivion of fear. But suppression itself tends to reach saturation point whereby its victims can no longer tolerate the oppression and they choose to speak out irrespective of the consequences. That is precisely what is happening in our times. Whether the formal institutions like it or not, women are going to find their way into the conference rooms where policy is drawn up; into the political chambers where values are dictated; into the ecclesiastical institutions where to date men have decided whether or not women are treated as equals. And if they are not allowed in, then they will use their imagination to circumvent the petrified institutions and diabolical systems, and create alternative ways of claiming their power.

What women are prepared to do so courageously (and in the eyes of many, so outrageously) is precisely the decisiveness which we all need if we are to bring about a better world for humanity and for our planet. The enslavement of the intuitive and creative spirit is a spent force that deserves finally to be crushed and destroyed for ever. The patriarchal powers are quick to retort with the well-worn clichés that we don't live in a perfect world, and never will! Not while the patriarchs run the show! It suits the powers-that-be to keep things 'imperfect' so that they can exert their whims and fancies, particularly over those who pose a threat to their unquestioned right to divide and conquer.

Devoid of imagination, human thinking easily succumbs to the forces of minimalism and idolatry. By minimalism I mean the blind dogmatism of the scientific method which claims that things can only be understood when they are reduced to their essential components (the divide and conquer mind-set). By idolatry I mean that arrogant self-righteousness that claims 'man to be the measure of all things'; hence, what humans claim to be the truth is automatically equated with the will of God.

That 'the whole is greater than the sum of the parts' is a scientific principle widely accepted even within the realms of mainstream science. There prevails, however, a deep-seated resistance to act on this principle; the cop-out goes something like this: 'Let's go on talking about it, experimenting with it, observing it under laboratory conditions; it hasn't been tested sufficiently to become a basis of our economics, our politics, our technology, or even our theology; let's move cautiously, when we decide the time is ripe.' What we really mean is that we are choosing not to allow the holistic vision to become a basis for those sciences where decisions are made that impact on people and on planet Earth on a daily basis.

You cannot conceive of the principle that 'the whole is greater than the sum of the parts' without employing the imagination. It requires a whole new way of looking at life based on intuition, insight, expanded consciousness, dialogue and creative experimentation. It calls into question the mechanistic, linear and political logic of the past 10,000 years. It rejects the old way of doing things; it resists the domestication of creative vision. It evokes a new way of being in the world, with people and with our planet, in a relational, co-operative mode beyond the destructive impact of patriarchal imperialism.

Resistance for justice

Herbert Marcuse once said that for an institution to be successful, it must make unthinkable the possibility of alternatives. There is a

will-to-power which drives all major institutions to be self-perpet-
uating; and to safeguard this development, institutions, and their
guardians, will go to great lengths to maintain the *status quo*. This
stance benefits the direct beneficiaries, usually a small minority,
directly involved in the maintenance of the system, and gradually
alienates the majority who frequently are the very people carrying
forward the mission of the system.

The call to resistance, therefore, is the people's call, from the
people to the people. It tends to be a grass-roots movement, essentially subversive in nature and veering towards prophetic
statement. It seeks a more just and equitable distribution of
resourcefulness, especially of power. To achieve this end it may
seek expression in all or some of these strategies: *conscientisation,
active protest, loyal disobedience, alternative communities.*

Conscientisation refers to the educational process of changing
perceptions, understandings and attitudes in favour of a more
holistic, open and creative view of reality. It is a process deemed to
be necessary to counteract the warped, controlled nature of information disseminated by the official organs of church and state, all
of which are committed ultimately to preserving and fostering the
agenda of the *status quo*; formal educational systems also are
deemed to be heavily slanted in favour of the official policy of the
governing institutions.

Media, on the other hand, while often critical of mainstream
institutions, tends to foster a consumerist, sensationalised view of
reality which ultimately deceives and misleads. Conscientious
objectors seek to highlight the fundamental limitation and injustice
of the governing system, whether it be within a family, a nation or
a multi-national corporation. Its target of criticism is the underlying tendency which seeks to maintain and preserve the *status quo*.

A spiritual vision for our time cannot ignore the overwhelming
power of information in our world today. Information is the new
power accessed with increasing competence and sophistication
through computers and electronic communications. Spreading the
word of Good News in such a world requires the ability to critique
in a creative way the forces at work, for good and for evil.

Active protest. A critique based solely or chiefly on words lacks
the realism and urgency required to activate a desired change.
The patriarchal mode often offers verbal denunciation without
the accompanying action to set injustices aright. Words can be

deceptively impressive, often bedevilled by collusion and usurption of power rather than forwarding the cause of justice. Feminist urgency pushes towards a more explicit statement, beyond the rational platitudes towards the 'irrational' embodied statement of disagreement and protest.

Protest involves a more embodied and visceral ('gutsy') commitment to those values and ideals we aspire towards or deeply believe in. I am prepared to put myself on the line for those convictions I hold dearly. Whether in a protest march, a sit-in, a lobbying of parliament or local government, I choose to act in a more passionate way, voicing and embodying my disapproval of the way things are and evoking an impassioned desire for a changed reality.

Protest offends against the respectability of our patriarchal 'niceness'. Protestors are frequently labelled as leftish, extreme or militant. Such scapegoating is a popularly deployed strategy of our oppressive patriarchal culture. Stepping out of line, going against the norm, is something we neither appreciate nor, if at all possible, tolerate. The right to active protest, and more importantly, the duty, is something we need to preserve and foster within a renewed spirituality of our time.

Loyal disobedience. To many Westerners, and to spiritually informed people in particular, this concept sounds threatening and bombastic: if you are disobedient, you are automatically disloyal! This simplistic perception arises from a subtle but potent movement in our world whereby we try to cow people into submission, control them in their submissiveness, and try to make them feel guilty when they strive to change that oppressive situation.

Loyal disobedience seeks to undermine the 'divine' right of any and every man-made system to lord it over others in an unquestioned way. Every human system can and should be questioned on a regular basis. In that way we keep systems open to new life and to fresh possibility; without that option many of our institutions are likely to become archaic and oppressive regimes.

Loyal disobedience operates on the understanding that truth arises from creative dialogue and not merely from those who make and superimpose rules and regulations. In an egalitarian culture everybody has a right and a duty to participate. It is from the cumulative wisdom of all, including the space for disagreement and even dissent, that we continually evolve ways of living and acting that do greater justice to person and planet alike.

Alternative communities. Patriarchal cultures tend to prefer the monolithic approach: the one system within which everybody operates; in that way, we know where we stand with each other. Creative cultures, and particularly spiritually inspired ones, seek to embody and respect diversity and creativity. This requires not one but several models for interaction, interdependence and mutual engagement.

A culture or system which outlaws any possibility for alternative modes automatically becomes an oppressive regime. Both people and the planet we inhabit require creative diversity to function meaningfully. We are creatures of many gifts in a richly endowed universe. We thrive when there is space, scope and context to explore and experience our diversity; in this way we become aware that we are co-creative creatures inhabiting a co-creative universe, invited to work co-operatively with our co-creative God.

Proffering and promoting alternative modes proves immensely threatening to every *status quo*, particularly to the political and ecclesiastical establishments. It undermines the patriarchal will-to-power that assumes and expects to have exclusive and unquestioned domination, often in the name of one or other monotheistic God-figure. It also evokes a subconscious fear that if we entertain alternatives the whole system might crumble to pieces which, of course, highlights that every patriarchal system is essentially precarious and fragile in nature; it is the blatant denial of that fact that makes many institutions so inflexible, and that requires alternative communities as catalysts for a more creative and hope-filled future.

Solidarity with the marginalised

Feminists seek a whole new way in which to exercise power. Today, everybody seeks to foster the notion of empowering others, but people differ widely on an effective strategy to activate and implement this new vision.

The prevalent model is that empowering is done from the top down; even contemporary forms of management still adhere to this model, camouflaged in a power-shift from top to middle management, but still a distinctly hierarchical system. Across the world there are several, grass-roots programmes intended to empower people to act locally to their own advantage; once again, many of these attempts are based on a superior wisdom from an external source. Some work, but many eventually fail, because they have not been grounded in the native, local experience.

The solidarity I write about here is one of a more complex and paradoxical origin. It begins with the experience of marginated people themselves. People begin to tell their own stories, their struggles and hopes from within their context and experience. They may draw on political systems or religious beliefs to help them articulate their struggles and their hopes, e.g. many liberation movements of South America draw on Christian faith principles and Marxist analysis without any of the ideological confusion that Christians and/or Marxists fear. Engaging in the shared story is the first major component of the solidarity journey; in itself, this may take a long time.

In due course the story itself begets an unease and a creative restlessness, an awareness that things should not be the way they are and that they could and should be better. This is where divergent opinions may ensue and another level of solidarity is required. People will need to talk, and talk, and talk; skills of conflict resolution and creative ritualisations may be needed to release the creative energy that is pushing the group towards the next stage of action.

The action may be one of passive resistance or violent confrontation, perhaps a mixture of both. The moral guidelines here have to arise from within the 'journey-in-solidarity' itself. Intuitive wisdom and gut reaction are often the guiding values and perhaps the most authentic for this situation. The risk of getting it wrong is only one of several risks being taken in this strategy. It is often labelled as a prescription for anarchy, descriptive – I suggest – more of the fear of the external observer rather than of the engaging participant.

What I describe here is a prescription for a whole new way of being political, one that arises from the experience of women's consciousness and of many marginalised peoples around our world. What I wish to highlight is that we are not dealing with an irrational desperate strategy of trapped, frustrated people who have no better recourse to 'constructive' action; we are witnessing a whole new way of being political; a counter-cultural engagement of solidarity and hope that provides a real sense of future not merely for the marginalised but also for those of us trapped in the respectible but equally oppressive regimes of outdated patriarchy.

Beyond respectability

Mainstream spirituality spawns a popular stereotype of the sub-
missive, God-fearing, ascetical individual, who is so 'anti-
the-world' in attitude and behaviour that the world can conveniently and justifiably ignore the challenge. Sometimes, the
stereotype (mistakenly called the archetype at times) veers towards
the heroic, of which Mother Theresa of Calcutta, Nelson Mandela
of South Africa, or the Dalai Lama may be considered modern
examples; such people tend to become so exalted in the popular
view of spirituality that we feel we never can and never should try
to emulate them. Their heroism becomes one pole of a dualism, the
other being one of powerlessness and worthlessness. Our culture
also tends to enculturate such people in formalised, supportive systems, e.g. the church, a religious system (Buddhism in the case of
the Dalai Lama) or even a mainstream political organisation (as in
the case of Nelson Mandela); this can exacerbate the distance (in
terms of spirituality) that we can feel between ourselves and such
inspirational figures:

> Heroes show us who we are not. Helpers show us who we are.
> . . . Heroes diminish our senses of relational, or shared, power.
> Helpers call us forth into our power in relation and strengthen our
> senses of ourselves. . . . Heroes have brought us causes and cru-
> sades, flags and battles, soldiers and bombs. As our liberators and
> leaders, popes and presidents, bishops and priests, shrinks and
> teachers, mentors and gurus, heroes have brought us pipedreams
> and smokescreens and everything but salvation. And this, I am
> persuaded, is because we tend to search everywhere except among
> ourselves-in-relation for peace. (Heyward, 1989, p. 11)

The spirituality unfolding in today's world is bottom-up spirituality; it is a spirituality of 'hands on', getting not just our hands, but
our faces, dirty as we struggle at the coalface of the brutal and cruel
world of our time. Struggle is a key word for a contemporary cred-
ible spirituality. It remains phoney and unreal if not rooted in the
real issues of the human struggle to grow and to be wise, to learn
and to love. In a special way it seeks to engage with the cultural,
political and economic forces which fuel the fiercely competitive
and manipulative world in which we live; even those who operate

this system often question its meaning and purpose, but devoid of a spiritual context are often at a loss on where to carry such questions, and usually drop them before dealing with them in any kind of a meaningful way.

Feminists are among the leading spiritual catalysts of this new awakening. They throw the questions hot and heavy; there is little they leave unquestioned, and that in itself poses a huge threat to our numbed culture of respectability. Beyond the questions, however, they offer a critique which is much more holistic and profound than that offered by any other cultural or religious source. They go beyond symptoms to causes: historical causes, such as the rise of patriarchy; cultural causes such as the language and symbolic systems we have invented to oppress women and all minority groups; political causes such as sexism; religious causes based on ideology and idolatry. Such a thorough analysis of causes strips away the external scaffolding; it can demolish the 'foundations' into a heap of rubble; it can rock the credibility and respectability to a degree that the whole edifice may feel 'out of control'.

Our Western, religious and Christian cultures have developed highly sophisticated defence systems to ensure that this threat rarely rises above the level of ideas. But when the people begin flocking out of the religious establishments the infrastructure begins to shiver and shake; survival and security feel threatened; although the questions will not be entertained, they can no longer be ignored either. What is the point in having an intact system, if it doesn't nourish spiritual hunger, if it can no longer augment the human search for meaning?

As already indicated, our contemporary spiritual crisis is not one of atheism – on a global scale, the search for utlimate and transcendent meaning was probably never so virulent – but of ennui, an apathetic aimlessness, a wandering in the desert of archaic religious ideology, empty religious rhetoric, and insipid religious spiritualism. The religious co-dependency is breaking down, but co-dependent children are seriously depraved of imagination; all they have ever known is the monolithic, incestuous closed system which they abandon at the peril of spending the rest of their lives in a 'no man's land'. It often feels like a no-win situation: abandon the nest at the risk of perpetual estrangement, or stay within at the risk of never growing up.

Feminist spirituality is one of a number of contemporary movements exploring and offering alternative communities for those who wish to take the dangerous and risky move of stepping out. It may be a place of supportive friendship, a space for alternative worship, a protest group, or a more widely cast friendship network. More importantly, is the fresh context that is opened up, the freedom and challenge to voice and explore new questions (and perhaps old ones), fresh options and alternative ways of viewing and understanding our planet and our world.

Not surprisingly, therefore, spirituality finds itself incorporating areas of human meaning and relating which in the past have been totally relegated by spiritual discourse and subverted by religious ideology. Foremost among these is human sexuality, the spiritual challenge and context of which will preoccupy us in the next chapter.

— 8 —

Sexuality: the erotic power of spirituality

Our longing to be in each other's arms is growing stronger than our need to have a target for our hostility. We would like to come together again. But how? How do we, who are veterans of so much combat in the erogenous zones, learn to love in a new way?

Sam Keen

A dark and cthonic eros, split off and repressed by a society of workaholics, has returned to our broken world with a vengeance.

Robert Moore

The full splendour of sexual experience does not reveal itself without a new mode of attention to the world in general. As a means of initiation into the 'one body' of the universe, it requires a contemplative approach.

Alan Watt

IN THE MID-1990S, a psycho-sexual typhoon hit the Island of Holy Ireland. The underworld of sexual repression spewed forth flames of burning passion, scorching women and children in particular; storms of sexual rage rocketed ecclesiastical and political institutions, even bringing the Irish government to its knees in November 1994; the waters of erotic desire cascaded into villages and hamlets that had never known flood waters before. The Irish nation was stunned and numbed as tremors of earthquake intensity threatened the very foundations of sanity and sanctity.

Like all great historical epochs it has left us with archetypal stories which need to be cherished, narrated and recorded. Fred's story is particularly relevant to the considerations of this chapter.

A parable for our time

Once upon a time, there was a priest named Fred, a caring, loving and holy pastor, who worked in a Dublin parish. He was a quiet, reticent man, devoted to God and dedicated to the people entrusted to his pastoral care. He was also a deeply human man, who in times of weariness and loneliness sought human and divine refuge, sometimes in the contemplative quietness of his room or chapel, but on other occasions in the sleazy, erotic world of a gay sauna club.

With Holy Ireland gripped in the frenzy of its worst-ever psycho-sexual typhoon, Fr Fred made one of his visits to the club. There in the early hours of a Saturday morning, he suffered a massive heart attack and died. He received immediate spiritual assistance from two other priests and medical attention from a doctor – all of whom happened to be in the club at that time. Also present was a trickster (in the archetypal sense of the word) who seized the opportunity for notoriety and offered the story to the media for an 'undisclosed sum'. Within twenty-four hours, Fred's story obtained news coverage across the world. It had been a stormy night in Holy Ireland – and a busy one in the valley of the squinting windows!

'And the disciples asked: What does the parable mean?' The problem is that nobody in Ireland – or elsewhere – tends to ask that question any more. We have lost the art of story-telling but also the discernment of story-listening!

The media had a hey-day on Fr Fred's story; with parasitic indulgence, they sought to uncover every detail, which in itself did not encourage a discerning attitude. As far as the media were concerned Fred had to be a homosexual, something that shocked many of his parishioners and further perplexed the sexually confused of our age. It transpired that Fred was only one of a rather noble coterie who frequented the club, patronised regularly, and in order of frequency by lawyers, solicitors, teachers and priests. And therein, I suggest, lie some vital clues to Fr Fred's untold story!

Gay clubs of the type frequented by Fr Fred provide a discreet, informal and tactile environment where men can connect with dimensions of life that are undernourished or suppressed in daily life. The needs being addressed – emotional and psycho-sexual – have nothing to do with sexual orientation in itself. The central issues are those of intimacy, loneliness and disembodied living. Watch any of the TV depictions of the legal profession at work (e.g. the trial of O. J. Simpson in 1995), engaged in a cerebral battle of wits, trying to outdo their opponents and conjure up as quickly and succinctly as possible verbal counter-arguments to outdo the other. It all happens from the neck up, an intellectualised head trip that leaves the rest of the body starving (and, I suggest, screaming) for affirmation and acknowledgment. When one realises that many members of the legal profession also marry (or co-habit with) partners of that same profession, the deprivation is likely to be much more convoluted! Any human being who devotes so much creative energy to one realm of the personality (the 'head') is inviting revolt from the deprived parts (the 'heart' and the 'gut'). Ironically, and perhaps, perversely, society provides outlets for our neglected sub-personalities!

The gay cub scene is a compensatory outlet for our excessive headiness. It is an environment in which you don't have to use your 'head' at all. Everything – the sauna, the steam-rooms, the private cubicles, the blue movies – is geared to instantaneous exploration and expression of visceral, erotic, embodied needs. Explicit and exploitative genital interaction prevails, but not necessarily to the degree that is popularly assumed. I have little doubt that a piece of thorough research would reveal that elements like touching, stroking, kissing, hugging and embracing are the primary experiences being sought – to address at the subconscious level the primary needs that have been so painfully neglected.

Our sexual wasteland

It is because we have been so negligent about our psycho-sexual growth that we now find ourselves swooning in a sea of sexual repression. At the conscious level, we are all too keenly aware of the rapid increase of sexual abuse in recent years, of the prevalence of incest within families and promiscuity without. We are bombarded with lewd advertising, exaggerated levels of hedonism and an addiction to emotional fulfilment. We are inundated with the prospect and promise of being the perfect sexual partner who will leave no need unmet in a society that yearns for quick fixes and the end of everything that militates against perpetual pleasure.

We are also conscious of what might be described as a 'sexual elite': those that follow the societal norms within the institution of marriage and the family. In this context couples carry out their sexual duties and responsibilities – often with a great deal of love and tenderness – but all types of taboos may be lurking in the background, and a great deal is never spoken of, either between the partners themselves or to their offspring; there are many no-go areas! And it is not uncommon these days for such 'respectable' people to have other liaisons outside the formal one-to-one relationship.

And finally, there is the amorphous, chaotic scene of sexual liberalism, sometimes a rebellious reaction; at other times, a desire to transcend the norms and restrictions of the past. Right across our world, pre-marital sex and extra-marital relationships have increased significantly in recent years; gay and lesbian partnerships enjoy a degree of respectability formerly unknown; remaining with one partner for an entire lifetime seems to be becoming the exception rather than the norm. And the blame for such liberal values tends to be unquestionably placed at the feet of our modern lifestyle immersed in secularism, individualism, hedonism and promiscuity.

This scenario provides some evidence for what I describe as 'swooning in a sea of repression'. Despite the descriptive nature of this account, it is merely the tip of a proverbial iceberg. What is said is minimal compared to what is not said; what is seen and observed is superficial compared to what the human eye is unable to see; what the 'enlightened' wisdom of our time comprehends is the conscious dimension of a phenomenon which for the greater part is unconscious, and can only be properly and fully appreciated when we begin to unravel and engage with the unconscious material.[7] The vast unknown is largely repressed; it is more convenient not to know – because then we would have to take more direct responsibility for what is happening; and in the process of doing that we would be revealing so much about ourselves that we prefer to keep hidden. But the more we try to hide, the greater the danger that the whole thing will explode in our faces!

Our underlying assumptions

A contemporary spirituality that chooses to ignore or bypass sexuality is grossly incomplete. But more importantly, the emerging issues of contemporary psycho-sexual growth are themselves essentially spiritual, and are incapable of responsible treatment apart from a spiritual ambience. It is neither insensitive, irreverent nor irresponsible to suggest – in the case of Fr Fred – that the quietness of the chapel and the intimacy of the gay club touch on the same fundamental needs, and highlight the complex but engaging questions that a contemporary spirituality must accommodate and try to confront.

To undertake that spiritual challenge requires an openness, honesty and sense of wholism that we rarely bring to our perceptions of human sexuality. The culture of patriarchy – politically and religiously – has left us with an enormous backlog of ignorance and repression. So much of our sacred sexual story, individually and as a species, has been driven underground. Shame and guilt abound; the journey to wholeness will require a great deal of gentle dialogue, tender care and deep healing.

To unveil our repression – which I suggest is collective (or systemic) rather than personal – we may need to begin with some very basic questions: What is human sexuality? What is our sexuality for? How do we experience ourselves as sexual persons? How do we interpret and engage with that experience? And we need to ask many critical questions about our inherited sexual awareness, the attitudes, prejudices and stereotypes passed on to us from previous generations (courageously and comprehensively explored by Eisler, 1995).

The legislators of our contemporary world – political and religious – consider human sexuality to be a set of libidinal interactions whereby people (normatively male and female) become attracted to each other and form an exclusive, enduring – and if possible, permanent – bond. The desired outcome seems to be: a stable relationship, which is generally considered necessary for the full development of the couple and as the most appropriate nexus for the rearing and development of children. Various religions will impose other norms and expectations, usually to the effect that monogamous marriage and the institution of the family are perceived to be of divine origin.

The image of the stable relationship is, in fact, of relatively recent origin. Marriage as we know it today first emerged in the sixteenth and seventeenth centuries; the Catholic Church did not declare marriage to be a sacrament until the Council of Trent in the sixteenth century. Prior to that time people lived in more fluid, but committed, relationships, the main 'stabilising' factor being the rearing of children which took up most of the lifespan in a culture where people died much younger than in our times.

The institutionalisation of the couple relationship is itself instigated by the value-system of classical science and the industrial revolution. Everything came to be understood as if it were a machine and hence, all life was presumed to operate in mechanistic fashion. Thus, there developed a sense of human sexuality as a mechanical interaction between two people begetting a third 'object' called a child, just one dimension of what Weeks (1985, p. 8) calls 'sexual essentialism'. In this way, sexual behaviour became synonymous with procreation, a mechanistic view to which the Cathloic Church adheres rigidly to this day, and one espoused by other religions – especially the monotheistic ones – with varying degrees of virulence. When we examine the troubadour culture of the twelfth and thirteenth centuries, we detect a very different understanding and appreciation of human sexuality with the focus on its playfulness, joy and, perhaps surprisingly, its ecstatic, spiritual potential.

Our Western mind-set, and the accumulated wisdom it has engendered, is notoriously naïve about, and uncritical of, the mechanistic culture of the past few hundred years. Our culture and formal institutions (church included) are so saturated in 'mechanisation', with an accompanying educational system that validates this model persistently, that it is enormously difficult to challenge it, never mind try to undermine it. Despite all our spiritual rhetoric about man(kind) versus the machine, we still operate subconsciously out of a predominantly mechanistic value system.

Meanwhile, as many contemporary writers highlight, the model of the machine has worn thin; it is culturally and socially exhausted (although, by and large, we still cling on desperately), and it is crumbling all around us. Externally, we see this in the industrial sphere and in the demise of many mainstream institutions (including our churches and religious systems). What we fail to comprehend is that external change tends to be accompanied by (and often instigated by) internal change of equal intensity. In terms of the internal forum, the diminution of the mechanical modelling is more noticeable in the area of human sexuality than in probably any other realm of human behaviour. Anthony Giddens (1992, p. 167) provides a cryptic statement of our current situation:

'Genital tyranny' results from the fact that libido has been stripped away from parts of the body needed to participate in industrial behaviour. A resexualizing of the body, together with a renewal of the original meaning of eroticism, which is linked to aesthetic appreciation, is called for as part of future revolutionary change.

Beyond the procreation model

The understanding of our sexuality as an instrument for the procreation of the species dominated Western thought until the middle of the present century; the introduction of the contraceptive pill in 1951 signalled a changed understanding. People began to sense that there is more to our sexuality than merely reproduction, and without waiting for the 'legislators' they proceeded to experiment and explore an enlarged sense of what sexual interaction could be. Thus there developed an understanding that sexuality was primarily about the love and intimacy that two people mediate for each other's mutual upbuilding within the special relationship formally known as marriage. In 1962, the Catholic Church changed its theology of marriage in accordance with this ensuing development.

Gradually the neat, safe, distinguished boundaries of the mechanistic model began to unravel as humans sought to reclaim a new sense of what it meant to be sexual persons. Psychology and the social sciences generally encouraged the opening up of all those horizons repressed and subverted by the predominantly mechanistic culture of previous decades. People were encouraged to feel their emotions, moods and desires, to articulate them and nourish them through meaningful experiences. What nobody could have anticipated was the emotional overload that would explode as the repressed material of centuries spilt over in some wild and often frenzied reactions.

But along with all that shadow material, new light was also beaming into the long-lost realms of how humans articulated amd mediated human intimacy. It was noted, academically and experientially, that sexuality, for thousands of years, was understood to be a primary medium of creativity – of which procreation was merely one aspect; that sexual ecstacy was inherent to mystical experience (as in the Tantric tradition of the Far East); that erotic passion underpins humankind's most ardent efforts to create a just and caring society (see especially, Heyward, 1989); that sexual playfulness diminishes the destructive potential of human aggression; and finally, and perhaps most shocking of all, that humans throughout the ages, envisage the activity of the Gods predominantly in erotic, sensuous playfulness.

Thus, we found ourselves in the 1980s – and thereafter – launched into a bewildering world of sexual upheaval. Beyond the narrow confines of 'sex for procreation' (which in religious terms means 'sex without pleasure if at all possible') came the expanded horizon of 'sex for intimacy in an exclusive, heterosexual relationship'. It was a short step to the next horizon predicted by Marilyn Ferguson (1982) and others that a new age was dawning upon our world in which intimate relationships would be marked by breadth rather than by depth. A new trend began to evolve: the tendency to give sexual (genital) expression to any and every 'deep' personal encounter, whether heterosexual or homosexual in nature. Although widely practised, few people have had either the courage or willingness to name this last development for what it really is. In fact, nobody can venture its naming without feeling something of its paradoxical potential for both a depth of intimacy that few could endure, and a release of sexual libido that could reap havoc and unimaginable destruction for the human species.

For the remainder of this chapter I wish to propose that the naming of this new sexual agenda is a primary task and duty for spirituality. I suggest this for two main reasons:

1. Only a spiritual perspective – as I use the concept in this book – will enable humans to comprehend, appreciate and engage with the new sexual agenda in all its complex dimensions.
2. Without such a spirituality, we cannot hope to internalise and integrate the challenge of the new sexuality for ourselves and for our world.

Transcending the labels

As noted in previous chapters, the tendency to label is a primary control mechanism of our patriarchal culture. All labels are derogatory and judgmental in nature; they arise from what is assumed to be a higher wisdom, often validated by formal religion, and their primary purpose is to declare deviant and, perhaps, immoral, that which is being labelled. Labelling, then, entitles those who rule, to subdue, castigate, punish or even try to eliminate those who practise and uphold the unacceptable traits or behaviours.

People with a serious drink problem tend to be labelled as alcoholic. In its strict usage the word refers to an addictive 'sickness' over which the person has no real control. Consequently it is deemed to be a pathological condition requiring institutionalised

care (the psychiatric hospital) for its resolution and the rehabilita-
tion of the person (commonly labelled a victim) to a reasonably
'normal' way of living.

We are told that the 'condition' cannot be cured, but the person
can be assisted to eliminate permanently the use of alcohol and,
thereafter, pursue a meaningful life devoid of alcohol. Thus far our
focus is entirely on the individual person with the problem, whom
we commonly label the alcoholic.

Thanks to advances in the social and psychological sciences we
have come to understand this predicament anew; we now consider
the context of the person's life to be as crucial as the person him-
self/herself, and that the context itself may be contributing
significantly to the problem. Thus the immediate family, or even
the family of origin, may be playing a major role in the cause and
development of this condition. The real 'sickness' may be resting
within the family system itself, a dysfunctional family entangled in
complex behavioural dynamics, leading to the scapegoating of one
or more of its individual members. Consequently, there may be a
profound truth in the throw-away phrase: 'They drove me to
drink.' The resolution, therefore, of the drink problem may require
as much redress for the sick system as of the sick person; in fact, if
the dysfunctional system is not addressed the individual member
may never resolve the predicament in a truly satisfactory way.

When we begin to understand afresh the alcoholic condition
within the context of the system (family, or otherwise), we begin to
see the dangerous naïvety and fundamentally unjust oppression of
the label 'alcoholic'. When we come to the sexual realm we find it
inundated with convoluted and oppressive labels. The whole
vocabulary is distorted, destructive and crude.

Let's begin with the word 'sex' itself, used to describe one of
nature's and life's most creative and dynamic abilities, yet shrouded
in repressive secrecy, toxic privacy, lurid innuendos, verbal banal-
ities and manipulative advertising images. We have taken the
sacredness out of sex and, correspondingly, its thrill and meaning-
fulness. For most people the word refers to that repertoir of
emotional attraction and genital arousal that often – but not always
– leads to sexual intercourse.

The prevailing language carries a heavy patriarchal and masculine bias, focused on genital pleasure often confused with the
phallic need for superiority and domination (what Giddens, 1992,

describes as genital tyranny). Thus, a great deal of public perception fails to distinguish between sex that serves as a medium of intimacy and love (to varying degrees) in a mutual relationship; sex that is sought for emotional and sexual pleasure; and sex that is involved in an act of rape (or in the several abusive relationships that prevail both within and outside marriage), an indulgence that is all about power and not about pleasure.

Conceptually we divide sexuality into three dominant categories, effectively three labels: heterosexuality, homosexuality, and bisexuality. Psychiatry goes further and labels unacceptable sexual lifestyles with tags such as transvestite, paedophile, deviant, etc. Medically and politically we tend to accept the 'scientific' explanation for all these conditions. In fact, such explanations are pathetic attempts of our patriarchal culture to control and subdue dimensions of the human condition that need to be explored and understood in a much larger, cultural and spiritual context.

Sexuality as archetypal energy

Not surprisingly, therefore, a new genre of sexual literature is beginning to emerge; more accurately, is resurfacing from the ashes of the age of repression. A range of contemporary theorists, usually writing from a feminist, psychological or spiritual perspective, invoke ancient archetypal myths, especially from classical Greek literature, to explore and comprehend the new paradigm of human sexuality (see Boelen, 1984; Lawlor, 1989; Moore & Gillette, 1992; Moore, 1992, 1994).

To obtain a more holistic and integrated view, we need to re-situate the Greek Goddesses against the more ancient tradition of the Great Mother Goddess, who took to herself a great range of lovers, not to father children, but simply for pleasure itself. The intense and uninhibited enjoyment of sexual intimacy was itself a primary expression of gratitude for the goodness and enjoyment of life. It was a different quality of pleasure from that which we use today to exploit and desecrate both people and planet; the pleasure of the Great Goddess was a polymorphous type, spread throughout the entire body and not just fixated in the genitals as is often the case in the lurid eroticism of contemporary life.

The Indo-European invaders tried to suppress and destroy the power of the Great Goddess (see pp. 71ff.), an insatiable creative potency that keeps resurfacing ever since, and today invades our world with a mighty and timely vengeance. In the epoch of classical Greek culture, it looks like the Great Mother Goddess became fragmented into many lesser Goddesses, each receiving attributes that once belonged to her: Hera got the ritual of the sacred marriage, Demeter her mysteries, Athena her snakes, Aphrodite her doves and Artemis her function as 'lady of the Wild' (cf. Leeming & Page, 1994, esp. pp. 133–57).

Aphrodite and Demeter are frequently invoked in the feminist literature and psychology to understand afresh the sexual creativity of women. Aphrodite is the Goddess of love and beauty, known to the Romans as Venus; this archetype governs women's enjoyment of love and beauty, sexuality and sensuality; it cherishes both the intensity of pleasure and the durability of fulfilling relationships, along with the paradox of trying to hold both realities in one's conscious experience. In much of the patriarchal literature and religion, the aphrodite-inspired woman is considered to be a temptress or a whore, a tradition that predominates in both contemporary Christianity and Islam and has caused enormous psychological and spiritual damage to women, particularly in the past 5,000 years.

The complementary image often invoked in feminist sexual consciousness is the maternal, nurturing figure of Demeter, the Goddess of grain and agriculture, amplifying the tradition of the Great Mother Goddess as the woman of prolific fertility, birthing new life as mother to humankind, but also to planetary life itself. Despite all this creative power, she is also considered to be the most vulnerable of the Greek deities. Vulnerability, and the desire to integrate it more meaningfully, is of special significance for contemporary spirituality. A great deal of human woundedness is sexually related, and cannot be dealt with meaningfully without a whole new way of envisioning our sexuality, experiencing it more wholesomely and integrating it into our daily life-experiences.

It is also worthy of note that the Greek God of love, Eros, known to the Romans as Amor, was the husband of Psyche. The psychic domain consists of mind, intellect, spirit and all the lofty aspirations that arise from within. But that ideal spirited life can evaporate into thin air if not accompanied by the sensuous and amorous that seeks to befriend, relate and connect. Without the power of Eros – with its often wild and fanciful playfulness – the wisdom of great ideas never percolates into the world we inhabit. Among Christian writers, Brock (1992) utilises this idea with great imagination, suggesting that what was unique in Christ's life and love was its eroticism (including its full sexual significance) which is precisely what gave passion to both his love and his desire for justice.

Theorists, exploring the contempoarary links of sexuality and spirituality in men's experience (e.g. Keen, 1989; Lawlor, 1989; Moore & Gillette, 1993) frequently evoke the mythical figure of Dionysus, the God of phallic ecstacy, whose domain is often that of the sacred mountain where he entertains his female worshippers in voluptuous revelry. The phallus is one of the most underestimated and misunderstood spiritual symbols of our time (cf. Monick, 1987).[8] Ever since we chose to cover over and hide the phallic symbol of the crucified Christ himself, we have either been castrating male creativity out of fear, ignorance or (most frequently) through male oppression turned in on itself; or, we have been projecting our phallic thrust in the personal barbarism of rape (much of which happens in the respectable domain of the marriage bed), or the cultural barbarism of guns, scud missiles and the other phallic projectiles that cause such pain and misery in today's world.[9]

The phallus normally refers to the fully engorged penis, but it seeks to symbolise the archaic, instinctual libido, which propels a man's enthusiasms, including his spirituality. In their study of the Lover archetype in men, Moore & Gillette (1993, p. 76) offer us a fresh perspective on our understanding of male sexual energy (libido):

We believe that Libido is the profound and complex expression of love and the lover. The life-force that energises the archetype of the Lover cannot simply be defined as sexual energy, contrary to the views of the classical Freudians. Nor is the Lover energy a simple matter of life and death instincts – in an eerie way Libido strives, simultaneously, toward both life and death. While profoundly earthly, sensual, and sexual, and while pressed into the service of procreation, Libido also aims at a spiritual condition which can be described as 'cosmic consciousness'. Libido is at once a drive toward multiplicity – through discrete, finite entities which affirm, protect, and extend their boundaries – and an impulse toward the union of entities.

The re-emergence of the androgyne

The mythic Greek figures help to explain many of the changing behaviour patterns in contemporary sexuality; they also affirm the need to view those developments in a spiritually informed way. One of the more complex, but pervasive, influences in the psycho-sexual growth of many people today is that of androgyny, encapsulated in the ancient myth of the hermaphrodite, of which Plato (in the Symposium) is one of several classic exponents.

In the contemporary understanding of human sexuality, androgyny is considered to be the ultimate deviation in which a person is so sexually confused and 'undifferentiated' that emotionally the person doesn't know whether one is male or female. Although clearly male or female at a biological level, the androgyne experiences sexual feelings and desires in a way that transcends the clear-cut distinctions that we expect to prevail when our sexuality is well developed and integrated – according to the criteria and expectations of the dominant, patriarchal culture! A good example of a contemporary androgyne, is the man who begins to experience a strong orientation towards mothering and home-making to a degree that he would choose to give up a well-paid job in order to spend time with his children and give home-making priority over everything else. But, in fact, the androgynous development tends to be much more subconscious rather than conscious and, consequently, whether in a man or a woman, will often veer towards a more creative way of being, perhaps in some quite esoteric area of work or lifestyle.

The androgyne carries some very deep archetypal energies which many theorists believe link us right back to a primordial state of being where our essential humanum was one, single reality (cf. Matthews, 1991, pp. 132ff.; Singer, 1977; Trible, 1978, esp. pp. 98–99), with the erotic energy spread throughout the body – hence the unfortunate phrase 'polymorphous perversity' (Kilpatrick, 1975, pp. 125ff). To retain something of this primordial and original unity, people pair up as male and female in an enduring relationship, subconsciously striving to realise something of the original archetypal unity; perhaps, everything in the couple relationship needs to be reassessed against this background, which all the major religions acknowlege in one way or another, a phenomenon which seems to have a spiritual foundation of great age. Of course that same complementarity of the sexes prevails across the whole spectrum of life-forms and, as Teilhard de Chardin (1970, pp. 290, 291) has so convincingly stated, is the basis of love itself:

> Considered in its full biological reality, love – that is to say the affinity of being with being – is not peculiar to man(kind). It is a general property of all life and as such it embraces, in its varieties and degrees, all the forms successfully adopted by organized matter. In the mammals, so close to ourselves, it is easily recognised in its different modalities: sexual passion, parental instinct, social solidarity. . . . If there were no internal propensity to unite, even at a prodigiously rudimentary level – indeed in the molecule itself – it would be physically impossible for love to appear higher up, with us, in hominised form. By rights, to be certain of its presence in ourselves, we should assume its presence, at least in an inchoate form, in everything that is. . . . Driven by the forces of love, the fragments of the world seek each other so that the world may come to being.

This complementarity which prevails throughout nature, can also be experienced in the lives of individual members, in the case under consideration, in individual humans. We are well aware in recent years, of the destructive split between the masculine and feminine that has characterised our cultural modelling in the recent past (perhaps, since the dawn of modern patriarchy). The re-integration of these two values in each one of us is closely related to, and often the instigator of, the experience of fusion that we describe as androgynous.

This is not an aberration, but a contemporary dimension in psycho-sexual growth that seems to be very widespread, but grossly misunderstood in a culture that still retains such a functional and unspiritual view of sexuality in general.

Many people begin to encounter the androgyne within themselves for the first time when they seek to accept and engage with the bisexual aspect of their lives. Unfortunately this often leads towards the appropriation of a more explicit homosexual identity and lifestyle, because that is generally promoted as the accepted 'alternative'. Not surprisingly, therefore, we find many people, who have donned the homosexual mask, and have tried desperately to integrate it, yet remain restless, lonely and alienated within. They have come 'out of the closet' supposedly, but in fact, have ended up in an even more repressive prison. Herein, we encounter just one destructive manifestation of the new sexual agenda that prevails in our time.

In religious terms, the androgyne tends to veer in the direction of celibacy, and many people in various cultures who opt for a celibate way of life, either temporarily or permanently, are, unknowingly, carrying something of the androgynous archetype on behalf of humanity at large. I believe that an approach to celibacy which would seek to explore its meaning in such archetypal terms, has a great deal more to offer, theologically and spiritually, than the narrow, ascetical interpretation within which we try to explain the meaning of the celibate life. Confronted by the fact that celibacy may need an androgynous and archetypal explanation to comprehend its deeper meaning, it is not surprising that the current approach to celibacy can easily beget pathological behaviour like paedophilia and other sexual aberrations. We pay a high price for neglecting archetypal energies.

In a rather courageous and prophetic essay, Fiand (1987, pp. 70ff.) suggests that the evolution of contemporary spirituality is calling us towards androgynous ministry, a pastoral response that will seek to undermine the destructive forces of sexism, one-sided gender modelling, and work for more 'radically inclusive perceptions and responses'. Before we can ever hope to have such a quality of ministry, we need to undergo a conversion of heart that will enable and empower us to contemplate (see) what is really going on in our world, to comprehend its deeper meaning, and to discern its challenge for us personally and collectively as a human species. Herein lies one of the most creative and complex challenges for psycho-sexual spirituality in our time.

Naming our reality as sexual people

Many of the great religions, particularly Christianity and Islam, seek to diminish the significance of human sexuality, considering it to be basically the product of animal instinct. They claim that it is based primarily on the animal drive to survive that we have inherited from our ancestral past. Some go even further and claim that our sexual drives, instincts and desires are nothing more than the 'animal' within; in other words, sexuality has nothing to do with our humanity. Consequently, we grow in humanness (and holiness) by conquering this base instinct and transcending it as far as possible. The aberrations and repressions this strategy has generated are all too well known and widely documented; it is not necessary to repeat them here.

A spirituality that seeks to integrate our sexual identity and aspirations as human beings may have to begin at a very basic level. This seems essential to the process of naming which I suggest is the spiritually and culturally appropriate antidote to labelling. In our essential nature, we are all sexual creatures; in fact, our sexuality is an integral dimension of our personal and interpersonal identities; if I, a man, am in conversation with a woman, that very interaction activates (or is activated by) a set of biochemical responses in my brain and in my nervous system; if I am in conversation with a man a different set of responses is evoked. In all human interactions, I am unavoidably sexual. It is my sexuality that attracts me to others, or repels me from them, that creates the human warmth that leads to closeness and intimacy, irrespective of whether a genital feeling is evoked or not. In fact, all my moods, feelings and emotions are activated from within that libidinous, erotic and creative dimension of my sexuality. Without my sexuality, and its activation in my life, I would be fundamentally non-human.

My concern is not about a spirituality of sexuality. I am seeking to unearth a much deeper, more ancient and primordial wisdom that regards sexuality itself to be essentially spiritual, possibly the greatest single source of spiritual vitality in the human psyche. This requires us to reappropriate dimensions of our sexual selves either suppressed or repressed by the ignorance and oppression of our patriarchal past.

Firstly, sexuality is a core ingredient of the evolving process of becoming a full human being. It is active from the moment of birth (and in fact for some months prior to birth) until the day we die. Secondly, our sexuality is activated in all personal and interpersonal behaviours relating to our moods, feelings and emotions; it is not just about animal urges and instincts – a conviction fostered strongly by those who adopt a mechanistic approach to sexuality. Thirdly, it is – as many scientists have noted – entwined with well-understood biochemical processes in the human brain and in the nervous system, but by reducing it to that rational and quantifiable basis, we leave unexplained practically everything about sexuality that makes it so special – and so frightening – for us; we try to explain away rather than explain the inherent mystery. Fourthly, it is – as Freud and others have highlighted – an amorphous and insatiable creative force forever seeking attention and expression, which I wish to suggest is primary evidence for its divine origin and not for its animal unruliness.

Above all else, sexuality is not a static entity, that we assume must remain relatively unchanged since its biological structure and function have not been modified for millennia. Sexuality is primarily an archetypal energy that co-evolves with the many other complex and creative dynamics of evolution at large. That change is largely internal and not external; it is a change felt and perceived in the inner realms of the human–planetary personality. The collective unconscious (in the Jungian sense) and the personal subconscious are probably the major influencing factors, with the former providing the unique spiritual power I write about in this chapter.

Reconnecting with archetypal meaning

Evola (1983) documents at great length how humans in ancient times understood their sexuality as a mode of interaction with the divine power itself. He concludes:

> Traditional man(kind) sought to find the secret and essence of sex in divinity itself. In his eyes, before physical embodiment the sexes existed as super-individual forces and transcendental principles; before appearing in 'nature', they existed in the realm of the sacred, the cosmic and the spiritual. And in the manifold variety of divine figures differentiated as Gods and Goddesses, man(kind) sought to understand the essence of the eternal male and eternal female which the sexual natures of human beings reflect and manifest. (Evola, 1983, p. 115)

Without invoking and pursuing this divine dimension, we cannot hope to treat comprehensively and holistically the various expressions and manifestations of sexual interaction that characterise human life down through the ages, and particularly in our own time. Nor can we hope to name appropriately and responsibly the meaning and desire of our vocation to be creative, sexual human beings. As we attempt to name our reality, in its diverse and poly-morphous nature, we hope to be able to dispel the destructive power of the dominant labels, and duly release the shackles of repression that create so much sexual pathology in today's world.

Anthropological evidence (see especially Eisler, 1995), uncover-ing our historic story as a human species suggests that long before marriage and modern morality ever came to be, people interacted and related sexually in a caring, loving and responsible manner. Evidence from ancient Indian and Chinese cultures strongly aug-ments the notion that sexuality was a power of the Gods entrusted to humans; for the Chinese particularly, its cosmic significance always took priority over its personal and interpersonal appropria-tion (see Bullough, 1976, pp. 281–310; Tannahill, 1980, pp. 169ff). The encompassing life-force took priority over the functional and instinctual drives of humans.

Consequently, sexuality was perceived to be, first and foremost, a spiritual force given primarily for the purposes of creativity. And it was a gift to be enjoyed, an engagement of ecstasy and pleasure that was understood to be a dimension of the 'divine delerium' itself. Mystics of these ancient cultures developed sophisticated techniques of sexual intimacy, prolonging the arousal and pleasure, in order to enter more deeply into intimacy with the divine life-force itself; the Tantric and Kundalini traditions retain many examples of this development; ancient Chinese and Indian art also witness to the extensive use of sexual engagement for spiritual growth and development.

Consequent upon this spiritual approach, there developed an understanding of sexuality as being primarily a creative force, aligning humans with their co-creative God, the God who ani-mated trees, flowers, animals, nature, and humans themselves in their relationship with creation, with one another and in their power and capacity to beget new life. But procreation was perceived as only one – albeit an important – dimension of the power of human sexuality.

In fact, our prehistoric ancestors, throughout the Paleolithic and Neolithic era seem more concerned about fertility rather than about procreation. According to Evola (1983, pp. 10ff.), 'the instinct for reproduction and the very survival of the species, do not in any way represent the primary fact; they are mere derivatives'. As indicated in previous chapters, the dominant theme of Ice Age art is that of fertility; many of the figurines are those of women in pregnancy or in the process of giving birth. It has been suggested in the past that this is evidence of the precarious nature of life in those primitive times when people felt totally dependent on the Gods for their sense of security; I don't know of any contemporary researcher who would agree with that interpretation.

The consciousness of being fertile people in a fertile world was itself a dimension of a spiritually-based view of the world, a universe in which humans co-create with a co-creative God. Within that framework, sexuality seems to have been viewed not so much as a biological or reproductive faculty, but as a dimension of erotic engagement with God's own erotic creativity.

Tangible evidence for these ideas is substantially available in the myths and artistic traditions of ancient Hinduism. Gods embracing in voluptuous erotic embrace are commonplace, and even to this day the joy and pleasure of sexual intimacy is considered to be a primordial spiritual experience. The guilt, shame and toxic secrecy that are so widespread in the Western world – the alternative extremes of promiscuity and lurid pornography – are largely unknown in ancient Hindu culture. Some contemporary writers are quick to describe and dismiss a great deal of this ancient praxis as 'sacred prostitution'; one wonders to what extent might this be a moral projection from the present onto the past and, like many such projections of the past hundred years, likely to be disproved rather than substantiated in the light of ongoing research.

Research into the Christian understanding of human sexuality highlights the negative impact of St Augustine in particular, who after a life of sexual frolic switched to being very prudish and judgmental of sexual behaviour. It is probably unfair to isolate St Augustine either in arguments for or against a strict sexual morality; Augustine reflected a prevailing Christian ethic which, although biblically tolerant and largely non-judgmental, quickly became a major religious and moral focus against the body, the legitimate pleasures of life, the imagination, women and finally against the created order itself (see the comprehensive study of Brown, 1990). This 'moral high ground' associated with Catholicism in particular needs to be assessed in the larger cultural context of patriarchy, which under both Greek and Roman influence had now become a major philosophical, political and economic force. Religion, and particularly Christianity, as the religion of the empire, was unlikely to escape its obnoxious influence.

The value system of Christendom (as distinct from that of Christianity) has had a major impact on the evolution of European culture and in due course on global civilisation as well. However, the dominant moralistic approach to sexuality, which prevailed from early Christian times, does not seem to have had as pervasive an effect, as the later mechanistic modelling of the sixteenth and seventeenth centuries. It was this oppressive regime that the Christian missionaries brought to many parts of the world, and with it a sexual morality devoid of the spirituality and creativity that seems to have prevailed for thousands of years previously. With the emergence of Freudian psychology in the early twentieth century, and its almost paranoid fear of the erotic, the forces of moralism dictated practically all the sexual mores – but none more sinister and tragic than the enormous repression which is now irrupting all around us.

Textbooks on the history of sexuality – and our human understanding of it – often begin with the work of Sigmund Freud and the application of his theories as outlined in *Three Essays on the Theory of Sexuality* (1905). Works that adopt a more religious orientation may begin with the understanding of sexuality in the Jewish and Christian scriptures, but occasionally begin with St Augustine and his anti-sexual polemic. There is very little in the literature that even acknowledges an enlightened understanding of human sexuality prior to Christian times. The evidence which scholarship has evoked, and continues to surface, is extremely selective, restrictive and very much biased towards the dominant patriarchal ideology of subjugation and control, with a few notable exceptions, that of Nelson & Longfellow (1994) being the one I am most acquainted with.

Erotic missioning

We are at a new moment in the evolution of human sexuality, a *kairos* that requires a deeply contemplative stance, if we are to comprehend authentically where the creative Spirit is seeking to lead us. The emphasis in contemporary culture, the one I have largely followed in this chapter, is towards overtly expressing our sexual yearnings and desires. I emphasise this dimension because it has been so neglected and undermined in the mechanistic culture of the past 400 years. In a sense, it is only when this dimension has been affirmed and appropriated afresh that we can hope to reclaim the underlying values of ancient ascetical ideals and, consequently, complement the contemporary desire for transparency with a sense of integrity and self-discipline that will enable us to channel and express our sexuality in creative and responsible ways.

Because our sexuality is such a powerful, primordial energy, both at the personal and societal levels, it needs to be protected by personal responsibility, moral guidelines and institutional contextualisation. It needs to be acknowledged and respected for what it is: a mystical, creative energy forever seeking articulation and expression in our creative universe. True creativity is beyond all human norms and controls and the challenge of our own creativity is to integrate (rather than tame) this radical freedom, to our own advantage and that of all creation. We can also draw on the wisdom of ancient times for practical guidelines in this undertaking.

In the Tantric tradition, the joy and pleasure of sexuality is highly valued and allowed a great freedom of expression. Nonetheless, there is also a central emphasis on self-discipline: sexual energy must not be dissipated (i.e. wasted) on illusory fantasies or desires; sexual engagements must not be exploitative of the other, and sexual body fluids (e.g. male semen) must be retained within the heightened state of psychic (spiritual) awareness, rather than released. The gift of sexual intimacy is understood to be primarily for ecstatic encounter with the divine which itself engages permanently in the relational mode known formally in Christianity as Trinity, a concept that has parallels in many of the major religions (with the notable exception of Islam).

Ecstatic engagement with the divine, however, must never become an end in itself. The divine co-creativity is, of its very nature, procreative and proactive. It seeks to beget new life, i.e. a fresh sense of meaning, purpose, engagement, action and mission. From the womb of divine becoming we are expelled into the heart of creation, but always with the reassurance that the one who missions us is the co-creative God(dess) of unconditional love. This generous and risk-taking love is the first and greatest gift we are called upon to bestow – upon each other, upon our planet and upon our universe. Without it, spirituality – in this age or any other – remains radically incomplete.

Spirituality and the collective shadow

I will state boldly right now that I believe we face a crisis – one of our own making – and if we fail to negotiate it with vision, we will lay a curse of unimaginable magnitude on future generations.

Richard Leakey

I tell you: One must still have chaos in one, to give birth to a dancing star.

Frederick Nietzsche

Abnormal thinking processes are especially evident in politics. Confusion is the norm in political rhetoric. . . . Inneundos, assumptions, vague statements, planned misinformation and suggestions are the stuff of the political world.

Anne Wilson Schaef

THE HEBREW SCRIPTURES speak of the God who will take from our lives the heart of stone and give us, instead, a heart of flesh. In the heartless world of our time, many wonder how we can reclaim a sense of heart for one another and particularly for the millions across our planet condemned to starvation, oppression, exploitation, poverty and escalating rates of violence to person and planet alike. Deep in our hearts many among us know that nature (and God) never intended us to live in such barbaric, cruel and awful conditions. Something has gone desperately wrong in our treatment of each other and of the life-forces with which we have been gifted; and increasingly we suspect that it is we ourselves, and not some forces external to us, that are at the root of the problem. We are the heartless ones reaping havoc and destruction on the very fabric of life itself.

Our fabricated spiritualities reinforce a great deal of the oppression and barbarity in today's world. We have invoked powerful conquering Gods, from many religious traditions, to subdue the nations for Allah, to suppress the forces of 'paganism', to bring 'civilisation' to the infidels of Africa, Latin America and Asia, to exonerate ourselves as a 'chosen' people, to segregate ourselves from the disrespectful peasants in case we become ritually contaminated, to bless and prosper our efforts to conquer and eliminate the 'enemy' who can be anybody from the infidels of the crusades, to the witch doctors of Africa, to the 'untouchables' of some remote Indian village.

Our spirituality is soaking in the stench of bloodshed, warfare, exploitation, peace purchased at the price of an armaments trade costing billions of pounds, blood-thirsty tyrants who rape, murder and maim, often in the name of a 'just' war, rampant injustices that gloat the rich and powerful thus condemning the poor and starving to a state of perpetual despair.

Barbarians within our own gates

Little wonder that we feel such an overwhelming sense of paralysis when confronted with conflict and suffering either locally or globally. In our arrogance, we are quick to name and to blame the scapegoats of consumerism, materialism, and 'evil forces'. I suggest the real barbarians are within our own gates, enculturated in the respectability and religiosity that is affirmed unambiguously by many of the 'noble' savages who uphold our official institutions of church and state alike. The great sin of our time – the outrageous injustice – is systemic in nature: the structures and institutions that are meant to be at the service of life, but more often than not fuel the forces of injustice, destruction and death.

There is no shortage of purported solutions. Political ideologies barter it out between capitalism and socialism, while in fact most peoples in the world are at the mercy of tyrannical despots. Religion still claims to have certain rights over the hearts and minds of people, most apparent in Islamic countries, but apart from these is very much on the wane as a cultural force. Economists hold the greatest power in today's world, reinforced by the unquestioned ascendency of the multi-national corporations and the persuasive impact of modern advertising; their solution is to overwhelm human desire in a market where human craving has reached saturation point, drowning out the desire and ability to pursue a life of meaning and integrity.

Whether it be politicians, economists or religionists, many people have grown tired and weary of a rhetoric that no longer cuts ice.

The verbiage of empty promises, whether it be the prospect of full employment (the greatest 'fib' of Western capitalism), zero inflation, diminished taxation or the guarantee of salvation in a life to come, only exacerbates our confusion and anger. We know deep in our hearts that the guardians of patriarchy are primarily concerned with their own comfort, security and survival. They don't understand the real issues; from their standpoint they could not possibly comprehend what it's like to live at the coalface.

Whether in the northern (the first world) or southern (the two-thirds world) hemisphere, humanity is currently sitting on a time-bomb, waiting to explode. Anarchy could be let loose at any minute. Indeed, were it not for the enormous energy and expenditure put into the enforcement of 'law and order', chaos would have broken loose upon our world reaping a havoc that is too frightening to imagine. It is this conundrum of human alienation, on the one hand, and planetary anguish on the other, that seeks recognition and redress today. Everything, and not just everybody, is languishing in meaningless suffering, the result of the addictive patriarchal urge to conquer and control, an urge now gone out of control and cascading towards its own ultimate destruction.

Confronted with such an ignominious picture – which I wish to suggest is not exaggerated and merits the utmost seriousness in a contemporary spirituality – what can we do, if indeed anything! People who are versed in the dynamics of addiction, compulsive or co-dependent behaviours, claim that the first necessary response is to acknowledge that one has a problem. Only then can the sickness be addressed, and possibly healed. Preaching a rhetoric of justice no longer cuts ice; just action, which fundamentally means a whole new way of being political and economic, is the only justice that makes sense to our suffering Earth and its peoples.

We are a threatened species

More than anything else at this time, we need to face the shadow of our own perdition: as a species, our days are numbered! In all probability, we are on the way out! We are a spent force, battling like hell to retain some degree of dignity and sanity but losing the battle at an accelerating rate. We may even be living in the terminal stage of a universal death throe.

It is a grim picture, but one we need to face. Not to face it at this stage would be grossly irresponsible. Ever since the publication of Rachel Carson's work *The Silent Spring* (1962), evidence has been accumulating that our planet is no longer capable of sustaining either the quantity or quality of human life that we are expecting the cosmic womb to sustain. At this stage the evidence is over-whelming – although largely ignored. I suggest that we are ignoring it precisely because we do not have a spirituality that would engen-der the honesty and integrity to confront it.

The dark night confronting us as a human species manifests in a number of different ways. The threat of nuclear annihilation is still very real, but because we are now much more aware of its cata-strophic impact, it is unlikely we will resort to that strategy. The irruption of rage and violence around the world is reaching epi-demic proportions; in itself it is unlikely to drive us to the point of extinction, but it is likely to make human and planetary life increas-ingly unbearable. The mechanisms of political governance and economic viability are in a shambles and almost incapable of resolv-ing even fundamental issues; just consider the pathetic reponse of Europe to the Bosnian crisis of the mid-1990s. A cultural death-wish seems to be irrupting amid the accelerating rate of emerging diseases and the diminishing impact of standard medicine (cf. Garrett, 1995). And in the midst of all this complexity, and the increasing sense of hopelessness, huge numbers, particularly the young, opt out and see no point in even trying to make sense of it all.

All these problems are grave, but even cumulatively are not likely to spell ultimate perdition for *homo sapiens*. The apocalyptic cloud of our age is an ecological one; we have so ruptured the womb that nourishes and sustains us that it has effectively become barren. The hole in the ozone layer, turbulent weather patterns, the strip-ping of the rain forests, the extinction of thousands of species every year, the gross exploitation of natural resources – are all manifesta-tions of a starving, screaming planet no longer capable of satisfying the insatiable compulsions of the primary predator, *homo sapiens*.

But most serious of all, is the state of the circulatory system of planet Earth itself: our rivers, lakes and oceans are now so polluted that it may be only a few decades until the production of oxygen itself comes under the threat of extinction. Even a small diminution of the oxygen supply will have horrendous consequences. With the death of life in our waterways, we'll quickly realise that interdependence is the foundation of all cosmic interaction; with the extinction of one dominant species we are all doomed, no matter how much artificial oxygen we try to create.

No doubt scientists will dismiss this prognostication as a lot of drivel, and politicians will try to undermine it with defensive rhetoric. Religionists will try to keep a semblance of hope alive by recording the saving acts of God in ages past. But all these panaceas suffer from the sin of shortsightedness, a spirituality of minimalism, unable to engage us meaningfully with this imminent hour of darkness.

Confronted with the demise of ultimate extinction, spirituality provides insight and understanding that seems unavailable from any other source. Although this wisdom won't save us from extinction, at least it will provide context for our reality as evolutionary beings and a realistic sense of hope as creatures of an evolutionary universe.

Confronting the sin of self-inflation

The contemporary denial of the imminent crisis is based on a grossly deluded assumption: namely, that even if planet Earth is destroyed, humans will somehow survive. This conviction is based on our patriarchal delusion that we are the superior species, with the superior wisdom and ultimate control over all earthly and global eventualities. Somehow or other, we'll resolve the crisis to our own advantage! This is our ultimate act of atheism and will prove to be our ultimate nightmare.

As highlighted in Chapter 5, the new cosmology purports a radically different view of life, one known to mystics for millennia. The primary life-force informing all living creatures is the creation itself in both its cosmic and planetary dimensions. From that primary co-creative source, whether one chooses to understand it as being essentially divine or otherwise – and spirituality can entertain both options – every life-form emanates. And no one life-form, human or otherwise, can be fully understood apart from that cosmic and planetary context. In short, the universe or planet Earth is not derived from us humans, so-called 'masters of creation'; we are the progeny of the greater life-force.

Moreover, the cosmos and planet that brings us into being are 'creatures' endowed with an intelligence far more enlightened and sophisticated than ours (hence, Fred Hoyle's suggestion of an intelligent universe). At this moment in time, we may be the most highly developed species on Earth, according to our own perception, but we are not superior to the Earth itself, nor to the intricate life-forces whereby the Earth survives and thrives as a self-organizing organism, having done so for billions of years before we humans ever came along, and will continue to do so long after we have been superseded by a more highly developed species.

The cataclysmic destiny, therefore, we are now facing, one that could strike before the end of the twenty-first century, will not mark the end of planetary life as many prophets of doom foretell; all indications are that it will be the end of *homo sapiens*, but not of planet Earth herself. The Earth Mother has survived global catastrophes before, much worse than that which is now impending; she will survive this one, too; and not merely survive it, but use it as the evolutionary basis for the emergence of new life-forms, better suited to the co-creative tasks of our new evolutionary moment.

And that forces us to consider the most disconcerting realisation of all: that planet Earth, acting out of its innate self-organising wisdom, is actually trying to get rid of *homo sapiens*, because we are no longer of any creative use to her. We are parasites sucking away her life-blood, belligerent and rapacious gluttons hoarding everything for ourselves, totally oblivious (it would seem) of the womb that begets and nourishes all we depend upon for survival and growth. It will probably not have been the first time in the evolutionary story in which planet Earth, in her unique wisdom, chose to get rid of wayward progeny and replace it with a more benevolent species.

From a spiritual perspective we need to regard the Earth Mother with the utmost reverence and seriousness. Beyond all the rational and scientific rationalisation, we, as spiritual creatures, must relearn afresh what planetary life is all about: not an object comprising dead, inert matter, but a subject whose wisdom and creativity far outpaces ours, yet – it would seem – invites us to co-operate with her in a mutually interdependent relationship.

Revisiting Christian Calvary

Those among us brainwashed in the pedagogy of Western rationalism could be forgiven for considering the above a lot of fanciful speculation, but those of us who call ourselves Christians cannot be forgiven so readily. Central to our faith is the Calvary and Resurrection experience, a paradigm of the process of birth–death–rebirth on which all life, personal and cosmic, thrives. The patriarchal compulsion to 'divide and conquer' turned human beings into robots long before computer technology was ever conceived. Consequently, persons are expected to be autonomous, isolated, self-contained and self-explanatory creatures. Little wonder that individualism is rampant in our Western world; the dominant philosophy of Western imperialism itself is the cause.

That same modelling of the human, as the unique, robust individual, we unconsciously project onto our divine figure-heads, whether it be the transcendent God of Judaism, Allah of Islam, or the Jesus of Christianity. In the synoptic Gospels, Jesus always points away from himself towards the new world order (the Kingdom) he is trying to bring about; Jesus does not wish to become the special focus of his own message. Christianity very quickly turns Jesus into the hero around which the whole drama takes place and then we proceed – in the history of the early church – to establish his absolute divinity, which for centuries thereafter tends to overshadow his humanity, and our own as well.

By individualising Jesus into the unique, divine hero sent by God, the story of God's New Reign on Earth, for which Jesus is the primordial disciple, quickly becomes the Jesus Story; the very context that gives prophetic edge, spiritual originality and cultural impact to the story is gradually undermined and virtually eroded. All the powerful narratives, e.g. miracles, become polemical 'proof-texts' to establish the divinity of this one, unique hero. The fact that the miracles are the first signs and tangible evidence for a new world order becomes a secondary consideration.

Gradually, the major events, e.g. crucifixion, become isolated experiences whose actual historicity we seek to establish to substantiate the existence of this one important person; we lose the archetypal meaning of crucifixion as a dynamic force that underpins so many processes in our daily lives and in our evolving world. In our attempt to personalise the whole message, we de-planetarise it. We reduce it to a patriarchal role-model which very effectively bolsters and validates the oppression and the injustice we seek to impose upon the whole of creation. This is a Christian rendition of our collective shadow.

To outgrow the negative and destructive power of that shadow, we need to learn to take extinction seriously. The most optimistic scenario we can envisage is one where we will somehow avert a global catastrophe, or if it does happen, somehow survive it. Our hopes of averting one are heavily reliant either on our self-understanding as 'masters of creation' who will engineer some dramatic solution or other (this stance is predominantly one of denial); or our self-perception of being altruistic, responsible human beings who will make drastic changes in lifestyle and behaviour in the face of impending destruction (this is very much a minority response and is likely to remain so).

The prospect of surviving such a cataclysmic event carries undercurrents of realistic hope, with the altruistic minority referred to above possibly playing a crucial role. The intelligent planet we inhabit is capable of self-organising to a degree that would offset the lethal effects of any and every major catastrophe, particularly to the benefit of those who are receptive to the Earth's own creativity. Historically, however, this has never been achieved (as far as we know) without large-scale destruction and extermination of the existing life-forms. Like the great Christian paradox itself, it seems that the radical newness of Resurrection-vitality requires the crucifixion of previously existing forms.

That being the case, why should any of us bother? Indeed, without the spiritual perspective, there would be no point in bothering, and I am not referring merely to the accountability we have to render to God at the end of life. Our spirituality is not about an after-life, devoid from this world, nor beyond it; it is primarily about engaging co-creatively with our evolving universe and the evolution of our cosmic home, planet Earth. The plight of the Earth is our plight also; the suffering of the Earth is our suffering too, and the Resurrection of the Earth is ours as well. Our choice to take extinction seriously, is a moral, cosmic and planetary responsibility, every bit as serious on a global scale as altruistic concern for my family would be on a local scale.

In fact, when we entertain, in a serious way, the possible extinction of our species, we either collapse into nihilism and despair, or evoke – maybe for the first time – the spiritual will-to-life, lying latent in the depths of our personal and planetary psyche. Then the shadow either becomes the darkness that destroys any possibility of light, or the catalyst for creative waiting until a new day dawns. To engage with deep shadow, we need to draw on all the resources we can; we begin to realise how richly resourced we are as human, planetary creatures. And for creatures so richly endowed, even cataclysmic extinction can have creative possibilities. In this resurrection space of creative imagination, even death itself can be transformed.

The shadow and chaos theory

The concept of the personal shadow and its implications for psychological growth and spiritual development is a topic which evokes widespread interest today. It speaks to many people's experience and enhances the human search for meaning. Many writers on the subject seek to expand the personal aspect and seek its application to other realms of life, especially in the social, political and cultural spheres.

In terms of a contemporary spirituality, I wish to acknowledge the immense value of this research and its contribution to human growth and integration. For the purposes of this chapter, however, my focus is on the potential and power of the shadow in its collective rather than in its personal significance. Light and shadow form the very basis of creation itself, at every evolutionary level and in all its various dimensions. It is in our ability to appreciate and accommodate this complementarity – on the universal scale – that we begin to appreciate something of the cosmic mystery that underpins and sustains life in all its multi-faceted elegance.

In our own time, many scientists (and economists) are intrigued by the notion of chaos, a topic we referred to briefly in the opening chapter. This offers a useful contemporary explanation of the shadow and its impact on our lives. Few of us today can escape the confusion and chaos that can erupt so suddenly in our work, in our relationships or in terms of our personal well-being. A kind of bewilderment characterises our contemporary world, one that baffles and jolts even the most sane among us.

The insights offered by contemporary scientists contain a great deal of spiritual wisdom. We are encouraged to embrace the chaos as an experience that can teach us important things about the meaning of life, and not seek to eliminate it as we popularly tend to do. In the scientific exploration, two schools of thought predominate: one invites us to explore the inner meaning, seeking out the patterns and possibilities that lie deep within the chaos itself, and for which one needs lateral imagination rather than linear introspection. The other draws attention to the destabilization which ensues when a system has exhausted its creativity and credibility, the chaos and confusion of disintegration, from within which the will-to-life throws up new possibilities often totally novel and unexpected.

Chaos theory is postulated on the premise that everything we see and engage with is living in one capacity or another; in an alive universe (see Chapter 4), life abounds and the more strange and mysterious its manifestations, the more authentic and real it is likely to be – all of which sounds bizarre and crazy to the patriarchal forces at work in our world, but not to those who seek entry into a trans-patriarchal world.

My use of the word 'strange' is conscious and deliberate. Open systems are often denounced for their amorphous nature, whereby everything is scattered and disintegrated; everybody does one's own thing; there is no sense of accountability; there are no obvious boundaries. These are valid criticisms, but unfortunately all based on overt observation and superficial judgment. When confronted with an open, chaotic system, the rational urge is to try and control the movement and sense of direction. Open systems respond much better to trust rather than to control. When we do trust the emerging system, and allow it its own time to unfold, a surprising thing begins to happen: something pulls the system into a new shape, which scientists call a strange attractor, thus allowing and empowering the system to behave in a totally new way, suspending its demise of total disintegration and projecting it towards a radically new and unexpected way of surviving. Describing the process in computer simulation, Wheatley (1992, p. 123) writes:

A strange attractor is a basin of attraction . . . pulling the system into visible shape. Computer phase space is multi-dimensional, allowing scientists to see a system's movement in more dimensions than had been possible previously. Spaces that were not visible in two dimensions now become apparent. In a chaotic system, scientists now can observe movements that, though random and unpredictable, never exceed finite boundaries. . . . The system has infinite possibilities, wandering wherever it pleases, sampling new configurations of itself. But its wandering and experimentation respect a boundary.

Other theorists, especially those who study complexity in the organic or chemical world (cf. Lewin, 1993; Waldrop, 1992), have refined the theory of chaos, postulating that the most creative breakthroughs tend to happen at the 'edge of chaos'. Chaotic, turbulent systems can be studied, and although their evolution is often unpredictable, recurring developments or measurements suggest that something new and unexpected is about to happen.

This has been noted by the mathematician Mitchell Feigenbaum and his associates in their observations that bifurcation – splitting into two new options – tends to occur when a process reaches a certain stage of development where key measurements are recorded. The 'edge of chaos', often perceived to be the moment of anarchy and outright confusion, can also be the critical point at which creativity is ready to explode. But in a culture so scared of pain, suffering and death, and so rooted in denial, we are rarely ready or skilled to engage meaningfully with the emerging possibilities. In a word, we don't have the spirituality to be surprised by the paradox of mystery!

A great deal depends on how we handle the chaos, and that in turn depends on who is handling it, and how enlightened they are in that endeavour. Illness, emotional breakdown or tragedy are human examples of chaos which we know can be so damaging that a person becomes physically or emotionally paralysed for life. However, many of us know of situations where people have retained their dignity and sanity in the midst of intense suffering, and not merely survived, but thrived; clearly these are situations where the chaos served as a contributory factor to a new lease of life that might well not have happened without the turmoil, confusion or breakdown. In fact, many of life's most creative, original and innovative breakthroughs emerge from catastrophic crises. In Christian terms, the radically new (Resurrection) seems to require a painful reorganization (or possibly, a termination) of the old, for its full emergence.

Chaos theory – which Gleick (1987) claims will rank alongside Relativity and Quantum as a major scientific disovery of the twentieth century – is another rendition of the power of shadow and its unique impact upon our times. It enhances our understanding of what is going on, but unfortunately reinforces our despair and despondency, because while highlighting the prevalence of shadow in our contemporary experience of the world, it also underlines the lethal forces of denial which prevent us from engaging with the chaos in either a meaningful or creative way. This adds to the grim prognostication for the future outlined earlier in this chapter. To choose not to engage with the chaos and shadow is our surest way of throwing ourselves at the mercy of the forces of darkness which will eventually destroy us.

Spiritual enlightenment – the ultimate goal of all spirituality – alone will save us from the perdition that could so easily consume us. Even if our destiny as a species is that of ultimate extinction – possibly before the end of the twenty-first century – the degree of spiritual awareness and integration is what will make the huge difference between meaningless extermination and a transformative crucifixion. Chaos, these days, is inescapable; whether it becomes an experience for potential life or for ultimate ennui, largely depends on the depth and meaning of our spirituality.

Reclaiming the daimon

For Christians, and those committed to the spiritual renewal of religious systems, a brief review of demonology (the belief in demons) may assist in understanding the reflections of this chapter and in integrating them into a more coherent spiritual strategy for our time. As indicated in Chapter 3, engagement with the spirit world seems to have been something spontaneous and reassuring for our ancient ancestors. The surrounding environment, the very air they were breathing, often felt like a befriending presence, something similar to what currently extant tribal groups describe as the power of daimon.

Daimon does not designate a specific class of divine being, but a peculiar mode of activity for which today we would use words like: genius, guardian, innovator, artist or trickster. Daimon is the veiled countenance of divine activity, but not a specific personification, and never associated with a cult or religious system. The daimon is considered to be an intermediary life-force between people and the Gods, the movement and force of creation. It is also considered to be the source of creative expression as well as individual destiny, befriending the people as they journey towards what today we might call 'divine fulfilment'.

Daimon tends to be viewed as a benevolent force, which will only affect people adversely when people themselves choose to ignore its power. What then ensues is a form of alienation which can manifest in ill-luck, sickness, misfortune, either in one's personal fortune or through the ill-effects of weather or nature. Being out of tune with daimon signifies being out of tune with both earthly life and divine favour. The psychologist Carl Jung views daemonization as the nurturance of soul, advocating our need to celebrate the earthly, sensual and ordinary experience of daily life, which may be neglected in a culture that over-rates the transcending power of spirit. Writers like James Hillman (1985) and Thomas Moore (1992, 1994) develop this thesis in much greater depth, applying it to the calls and challenges of our own time.

During the Hellenistic period, following the campaigns of Alexander the Great, contacts between the Mediterranean world and Mesopotamia, Persia and India, laid the groundwork for an elaborate understanding of demons, providing the basis for the complex beliefs that duly emerged in Judaism and Christianity. The power of daimon was fragmented and particularised in angelic creatures called demons, who progressively were endowed with greater spiritual prowess, with corresponding levels of fear among people. Initially, the demons were regarded as either good or evil, following the dualistic thought-patterns of the time; only in Christian times does the word demon assume a totally evil connotation. The culmination of the shift from the daimon to the demon is the inevitable personification of evil itself in the person of Lucifer or Satan.

The invention of Satan no longer provides the ultimate explanation for evil in the world; rather it validates a process of projection and scapegoating whereby we excuse ourselves from dealing more directly with the suffering and evil which we, and not Satan, inflict upon our world. Evangelical cults and sects invoke the notion of Satan and its divine power with a conviction and zeal that is both preposterous and idolatrous. Sometimes, the intention is to intimidate their disciples into infantile submission; in most cases the evangelical rhetoric about Satan ends up rationalising rather than explaining the meaning of evil. While we still apply the satanic description to certain 'evil' practices, the impact of Satan as the personification of evil seems to have little spiritual or theological significance for our world today.

Grappling with the problem of evil in the contemporary world tends to take quite a different direction. The complex, mysterious nature of evil and suffering is more readily acknowledged; the call to confront evils more directly rather than pray for their elimination features strongly in contemporary spirituality. It is, however, the growing awareness that most of the meaningless suffering in the world is caused by us, humans – directly or indirectly – that engages us most conscientiously today. If we humans sought to eliminate, or at least reduce, all the 'evil' to which we contribute, there is good reason to believe that we would not have a major problem (spiritually), in being able to live meaningfully with the suffering and pain that would be left (cf. Daly, 1988, esp. p. 167). I describe this as a growing awareness; the problem remains however, that the majority of human beings – spiritually and politically – do not subscribe to this point of view.

To this extent, immersion in the shadow, and denial of its reality, continues to be the great sin of our time. At both the personal and political levels, the destructive power of the shadow is rampant. This is particularly painful in the reckless projections of evil onto the many scapegoats we have invented – at the personal, political and religious levels – in order to escape the confrontation both with the darkness within and the evil we create without, often institutionalised in a series of systems designed to maintain eternally the power and dominance of patriarchy.

From paranoia to metanoia

Metanoia is the Greek word used for conversion in the Christian Gospels. It is the etymological opposite of paranoia, the psychological term which translates as intense, obsessional fear that cripples a person into emotional and even physical paralysis. The road to conversion is essentially one of outgrowing our destructive and crippling fears. Many of our greatest fears are self-made, convoluted psychological and political perceptions that assist in keeping patriarchal domination as intact as possible.

Most of us come into the world in a state of rage and anger, full of crippling fear because of the nature of the birth trauma itself. We assume this to be a natural process of nature, and theologically some still consider it an appropriate reminder that we enter the world in a state of original sin. Alienation is our natural birthright which will remain with us all our lives; many hold that it increases as life unfolds.

There is now substantial neo-natal and gynaecological evidence to show that a great deal of the trauma surrounding human birth is induced and caused by us, particularly by the barbaric history of male manipulation of the female body and masculine invasion of female fertility. Mary Daly (1978) vividly and gruesomely portrays the patriarchal degradation of female fertility as the science of gynaecology developed throughout the eighteenth and nineteenth centuries; she also illustrates the blasphemous interference of Catholic moralism depicting woman's suffering at birth as a just wage for the sin of Eve and for women's sins down through the ages. Little wonder that the birth trauma evokes so much rage in men and women alike!

Fortunately, we are emerging from this dark age of patriarchal satanism. Women are beginning to reclaim the sacredness of their bodies and the power of their fertility in its essential wholesomeness. We are much more aware of the need for pre-natal care and attention for the growing foetus, monitoring more vigilantly the psychological impact of the internal influences of the womb and the external influences of the environment. As mothers prepare themselves more consciously and lovingly for the birth experience, the traumatic aspects can be reduced considerably. New forms of birth, such as underwater birth, deliver and welcome the new-born into the world in a much more wholesome and pain-free experience. The journey from the womb to the world does not have to be the first dose of hell-on-earth!

Gradually, too, we are beginning to realise that we are born, not into an alien, but into a loving, world. We come alive because our world is alive, not because some inert substance is enlivened by a God-inserted soul. The world welcomes every creature, human and otherwise, as an affirmation of its own unlimited fertility. The elements dance with joy as each creature emerges from the womb, itself a microcosm of the planetary and cosmic womb.

Birth was never intended to be a frightening experience; we have made it so, and a primary call to conversion is to deconstruct the gynaecological monstrosity we have invented. With a more tender and benevolent entry into the world, our whole attitude to life, and feeling for it, will change profoundly. The journey from paranoia to metanoia then takes on a very different meaning.

As we grow up in a more conscious awareness of a loving and caring universe we gradually begin to see the stupidity and destructiveness of our denial. We are more readily disposed to reclaim our own shadow, to love our own fragility, to befriend our own struggles and those of others. We become empowered to break down the vicious cycle of fear-alienation-denial-projection-destruction.

It is only against this inclusive, ecological background that we begin to understand afresh that our human lives are fundamentally intertwined with the life of planet Earth and, in turn, with that of the entire cosmos. Apart from these interconnections and inter-relationships, our lives have no real meaning. Apart from that same planetary and cosmic ambience, we cannot hope to understand and engage with the power of shadow, human and planetary.

Throughout this chapter, I have given primary attention to the larger planetary and cosmic darkness, often referred to as the collective shadow. This is the creative darkness that begets birth, death and rebirth, at times manifesting in explosive exuberance, chaotic, amorphous but unambiguously fertile; at other times, manifesting in the destruction of decline, decay, termination and death. In the grand scale, everything has its place and its season; when we learn to embrace the trans-patriarchal vision in a conscious and contemplative way, we will have little difficulty in appreciating the elegance and mystery of its overall meaning.

The individual shadow needs to be understood afresh within the context of the collective one. Essentially, our struggles are those of the larger reality; our pains are those of a planet unceasingly in the pangs of birth-death-rebirth; our instinctual urges are those of that wild creative energy that floods our world with beauty and elegance, with the joy and pain of new birth. Our darkness, at all times, is impregnated with the confusion, fear, expectancy and hope that characterises every experience of Resurrection. Our search for a more just world order will never produce the 'fruits of righteousness' until we choose to befriend the larger context, the polarity of light and darkness that informs the whole of creation.

The greatest single challenge confronting spirituality in our trans-patriarchal era is the reappropriation of the shadow in all its dimensions of creation and destruction. And because of the precarious balance of the life-forces in our confused world, meaningful engagement with the shadow requires our most serious and most urgent attention. Time alone will tell if we can meet that unique challenge.

— 10 —

Spirituality and the Kingdom of God

The hermeneutics of the Kingdom of God exist especially in making the world a better place. Only in this way will we be able to discover what the Kingdom of God means.

Edward Schillebeeckx

The Kingdom of God serves as a focal referent for interpreting the diversity and constancy of how God acts in history. . . . In solidarity with those who suffer, Christian witness interrupts history – rupturing the structure of consciousness, the systems of oppression and the massive denials of human hope.

Rebecca S. Chopp

CHRISTIAN THEOLOGY, under the guidance and surveillance of the church, claims to supersede spirituality and provides the only authentic context within which the spiritual life can be studied or explored. In effect, this has often meant that the study of spirituality ended up in the hands of a select elite, usually members of religious orders, predominantly male (and white), and purporting a spiritual ascesis away from and over against the world of daily intercourse.

Saints and sages, mystics and philosophers have had reservations about this type of spirituality. Lecky's reaction to early Christian asceticism captures something of the unease which marks many epochs of Christian spirituality:

There is perhaps no phase in the moral history of mankind of a deeper or more painful interest than this ascetic epidemic. A hideous, sordid and emaciated maniac, without knowledge, without patriotism, without natural affection, passing his life in a long routine of useless and atrocious self-torture, and quailing before the ghastly phantoms of his delirious brain, had become the ideal of the nations which had known the writings of Plato and Cicero and the lives of Socrates and Cato. (*History of European Morals*, Vol. 2, 1911, p. 107)

One indeed wonders why or how could the Christian calling to love and compassion ever have led to such extreme and outlandish deviations. The prevalence and approval of such behaviours is only one of several indicators that our understanding and appropriation of the Gospel message itself has been distorted and deluded. The emerging theology of our time confirms this evaluation on several important issues.

Foremost among the theological ferments of our day is a desire to reclaim the Kingdom of God (henceforth referred to as the New Reign of God or the Basileia) as the primary data for Christian theology; the ramifications for spirituality are substantial and far-reaching.

Jesus and the Basileia

Christian believers have always attributed primary significance to the four Gospels, over and above other sections of the Christian scriptures. They document the life and vision of the founding person, Jesus of Nazareth. How much is historical fact or popular fable remains largely unresolved, but no longer remains the central concern. How we interpret classical texts, especially in the area of religion, is now viewed in fresh relief. We look for the deeper meaning not so much in the facts, but in the unfolding story which carries the mythical creativity and archetypal search-for-meaning in a much more coherent way than any set of facts ever could. The story, therefore, becomes our primary concern.

When we look at the Jesus story as it unfolds in the four Gospels, there is one outstanding theme, recurring time and time again: the Kingdom of God (Basileia), a phrase that occurs well over a hundred times and provides the focus for many of the parable narratives and for some of the outstanding miracle stories as well.

Adopting the strategy of story-telling – verbally through parable and symbolically through miracle – Jesus acknowledges the socio-political culture of the day, challenges it at times quite subversively, and works towards its transformation by providing (not just suggesting) a radically new way of living. Jesus acknowledges the role of the king in the prevailing culture, along with all the trappings of power and glory that go along with the role; he is also aware of the inherited Judaic wisdom that validates the kingly way of being by envisaging God as a king who rules over heaven and earth; what seems to have been particularly disconcerting for Jesus was the exclusive, oppressive and class-distinction regime that prevailed within the world of royal power.

Not only does Jesus choose to turn his back on the world of royal power and privilege, but he seeks to undermine its very meaning, declaring it to be fundamentally flawed and alien to spiritual maturation. He quite explicitly and subversively disassociates himself from the culture of kingship – in both its religious and political significance – and proffers a counter-cultural view: a new world order, marked by right relationships of justice, love, peace and liberation.

The daring and creative vision of the Jesus project can be gleaned from the following list, contrasting the earthly king's way of doing things with the way suggested by Jesus:

The earthly king	The Kingship of Jesus
Power from on high.	Power from the centre outward.
Power vested in a specially chosen person.	Power shared to empower everybody.
Power validated by the one, supreme God on high.	Power validated by the God who becomes incarnate on Earth.
The king dominates by a policy of 'conquer and control'.	The King serves by giving his life for the people.
Relationships are based on domination-subjugation.	Relationships are based on equality, justice and love.
The politics of kingship require social classes based on hierarchy.	A classless society of radical equality.
Rule by the force of law.	Relate through the power of value.
Power located in the exclusive sacred space of palace or Temple.	Power for the people at the heart of the world.
Only the elite can enter the royal/sacred space.	Invite in everybody!
Exclude all who are not 'respectable'.	Include all, especially women, sinners and tax-collectors.
You are paid according to rank and ability.	Everybody receives the same wage.
You get promotion by following the example of your seniors.	The tax-collectors and prostitutes get in before the righteous ones.

There are several examples in the Synoptic Gospels (Matthew, Mark and Luke) in which the disciples and admirers of Jesus want to establish him as their King. At all times he strongly resists this wish – except for one occasion, overladen with the prophetic power of symbolic subversion: on the final journey to Jerusalem (Mk 11:1–10; Matt. 21:1–9; Lk. 19:29–38). The people try to create the atmosphere of a royal gala and chant to the honour and glory of their King. On this occasion, Jesus co-operates with the tribute being paid to him and he does not ask the people to refrain from their royal accolades.

In this episode, however, symbol speaks louder than words; the acted out parable is much more audible and shattering than any verbal narration could ever be. To be true to the wishes and desires of the people – to be the type of King they wanted – Jesus should have been riding on a horse, as royal heroes had been doing for thousands of years previously. The horse was the royal beast, of power, elegance, glory and domination. The donkey is commonly understood to be the beast of burden, used by the ordinary people going about their daily chores, travelling, ploughing, threshing and carrying loads. According to Genesis 49:11 and Zach. 9:9, the King of the last time, who will establish a reign of harmony among the nations of the world, will ride, not on a horse, but on a donkey. With this prophetic and provocative gesture, Jesus is turning on its head the prevailing understanding of kingship. He is declaring it irrelevant and redundant. A radically new way of governance is being inaugurated.

One of the outstanding features of the New Reign inaugurated in the life and ministry of Jesus is an unprecedented sense of inclusiveness in a society where class distinction and exclusive privilege seem to have been quite common. Even a cursory reading of the Gospels leaves the inescapable impression of Jesus breaking rules and laws at random, ignoring the prevailing taboos, disregarding the solemn religious regulations, and stretching the boundaries of exclusion whenever and wherever possible.

That same fluidity, flexibility and inclusiveness seems to have prevailed in the early Christian communities, and in the initial foundations of what we now call the church. In the churches to which Paul ministers, formal priesthood seems unknown, mutual service and support, especially for the marginated was common, and the people seemed to relish and celebrate the diversity of their giftedness to and for each other. Not surprisingly, therefore, the church came to be understood as the servant and herald of the Basileia. (For further elucidation, see Fuellenbach, 1995.)

Domesticating the Basileia

But as Christianity grew and expanded, priorities became quite blurred. The power that Jesus so strongly resented and resisted infiltrated the growing body of believers. Although deeply imbued with the spirit of loving service to the poor and marginalised, and uncompromising opposition to the forces that dehumanised people and creation, the early Christians began to perceive themselves as a moral force that could battle for the cultural supremacy of the age. To do this they had to organise themselves into another humanly devised system that could stand shoulder to shoulder with the other dominant systems of the time.

They looked to Greece for the conceptual and linguistic structures (hence the tendency to divide everything into pairs of dualistic opposites) and they looked to Rome for institutional frames of reference (e.g. the vestments worn at Eucharist are modelled on old Romanesque dress). They developed a patriarchal priesthood, initially to preside at Eucharist, but within a few short centuries the priestly system sought to match the political emperor in prowess and control. And to validate all this, Christians began to work on their Christology, culminating in the famous diatribe of the Councils of Nicea (325 CE) and Chalcedon (451 CE) where the divine rather than the human face of God came out triumphant. Jesus became the cultural hero that could match and supersede any of the other great heroes of the day.

This was a long step from the Galilean prophetic peasant who took pride in washing road-worn feet, who shared bread with tax-collectors and sinners, who bound up the wounds of the abandoned Samaritan, who cherished the company and giftedness of women and who denounced the religious leaders of his day as whitewashed sepulchres. The hero depicted by cultural christendom had little in common with the first disciple of the Basileia; in the church today, they have even less in common.

By the time of Constantine, who accepted Christianity as the official religion of the Roman Empire, the imperial imprint had been indelibly stamped on the Gospel message. To mark the peace

of Constantine (c. 310 CE) Jesus was conferred with the title Pan-
tocrator (Lord of the Universe), in whose name the Emperor
inaugurated the millennium in which the Christian Messiah would
reign alongside his own emperors until the millennium had run its
course. Not surprisingly, therefore, after the Council of Chalcedon
(451 CE), the emperor issued an imperial edict that any officer who
opposed the dogma ('truly God and truly human') should be
stripped of his rank. The power of God's New Reign had been
usurped and domesticated; the prophetic cutting edge had been
virtually extinguished and would remain subdued far beyond the
duration of the 'royal' millennium.

Church and Kingdom (Basileia) were considered to be one and the
same thing. In fact, it was even worse, because Church appropriated
pride of place, and over the centuries the church tended to model her
mode of being on the socio-political institutions around her rather
than stand in counter-cultural opposition to them. Consequently,
when the church developed a just war theory, it was not with a view
to being a counter-cultural witness for peace and non-violence, but
rather to justify itself in playing war games with neighbouring political states. Litte wonder then that the church declared the feast of
Christ the King in the mid-1920s, imploring God to save the royal
families of Europe against the rising evil force of democracy.

Fortunately, our deepest values as a human and spiritual species
can never be eroded completely – because they are so fundamental
to our nature as spiritual creatures; consequently the Basileia, as a
constellation of such values, continues to resurface, time and time
again (see Viviano, 1988). Throughout the nineteenth century, a
number of European (so-called liberal) theologians (A. Ritschl,
J. Weiss, A. Van Harnack, A. Sweitzer, K. Barth, F. D. Maurice)
evoked a renewed interest in the significance and meaning of the
Basileia. It was not until the 1960s, however, that the Basileia came
to be understood afresh as the heart and core value of the Christian
faith; this momentum has come as much from spiritual writers as
from formal theological research.

To rule or to relate?

Modern spirituality confronts the Christian community with the
urgent need to retrieve the subverted vision of God's New Reign.
The challenge arises not just from within Christianity itself as its

increasingly disillusioned membership voice their discontent about the role of Christian witness in today's world. It is in fact the world itself that is seeking to reclaim the vision of the Basileia, because that vision speaks so cogently to the critical questions of our time. Foremost among such questions is the call to a new quality of relatedness at every level of life.

In the culture of Christ's time all relationships were characterised by hierarchical ordering and graded significance on the patriarchal ladder of masculine power. To make the system work, values such as inequality, exclusiveness, class distinction, independence and dependency were considered to be indepensible. To validate the system, God was invoked as the fatherly figure on top of the patriarchal ladder; humans, especially men, were perceived to be his first-born creatures, who claimed for themselves unique access to God's will over and above all other beings who inhabited planet Earth. Relationships, therefore, were deemed unique to humans only! And in the eyes of the governing patriarchs, the system could have worked to perfection except for the misguided influence of women. They, more than anybody else, should be excluded and suppressed.

Jesus confronts that culture with the verve and vision of prophetic proclamation. He denounced the oppression, pronounced its demise – to the cost of his own life – and inaugurated a whole new scheme of relationships. In the new mode of relating the key qualities are: *inclusiveness*: everybody, at all times and in all situations must be included and not excluded; *equality*: there is no status or class distinction in the Basileia where all are paid equally whether they arrive at the first hour or at the eleventh; *justice*: in which everybody is accorded a fair share of goods and resources to live with dignity and equality; *liberation*: from all forms of oppression and slavery, within and without; *peace*: harmony within the heart, within the home, within the community and within the planet ('happy are the gentle for they shall inherit the Earth'); *love*: the ultimate value that makes all the others possible.

In proclaiming the power and message of the Basileia, Jesus was not offering something to be realised at some future 'eschatological' time or in some other utopian place beyond this world. No, the New Reign of God is already at work in the here and now, and can be evidenced as we see the blind being restored to sight, the deaf hear and the dumb have their tongues released, the slaves are set free and the marginalised are included even at table-fellowship itself (the supreme sign of inclusiveness in that culture). The most frequently used verb in the Gospels to describe the engagement with the Basileia is 'entered' (cf. Harrisville, 1993, p. 143). Jesus was not proclaiming some utopian dream for the end-time, but a transformative personal and political experience of the now and open-ended future, not something to be subjected to pious plati-tudes or even to theological rhetoric, but something to be lived with all the passion and commitment that humans could muster.

Many Christians today – perhaps, the disillusioned more than anybody else – yearn afresh for the vision of the Basileia. Christen-dom carries the dead weight of a sacred tradition, but one that has outlived its usefulness, and in its decline and disintegration, con-fronts the Christian community with some fundamental questions of meaning. Foremost among these is the retrieval of the Basileia as the heart and centre of our Christian faith. Such a venture poses serious and profound questions about the Christian tradition itself: can we be sure that Jesus wanted his vision channelled into a denominational church (see Denaux, 1996)? More relevant to the considerations of the present work: can we assume that Jesus actu-ally wanted a new religion in his name? Could it be – as Sheehan (1986) asserts – that Jesus wanted to get rid of formal religion – all religion – so that we could engage afresh with the 'fullness of life' that the Gospels invite us to embrace? Could it be that the con-temporary desire for spirituality-beyond-religion was already pre-empted in the life and vision of Jesus?

Such questions cast the multi-faith dialogue into fresh relief, because the aspiration for right relationships, which is at the heart of the Basileia vision, is also a key value in all the major religious systems. As we each get to the deep story of our respective faiths, beyond the accretions and empty rhetoric of calcified tradition, we are likely to discover values that belong not just to the great reli-gions but to the primordial dreams and archetypal values of humanity at large (broadly, the approach adopted by Knitter, 1995). Our religion may be the local harbour that points to the vast ocean beyond, without which the harbour would never exist in the first place. By clinging desperately to our unique tradition, we may, in fact, be choking it to death, depriving it of the life-source that brings it into being in the first place and without which it becomes an empty caricature devoid of vitality and hope!

The Basileia and spirituality

It seems as if Christian theologians are only at the early stages of this new theological exploration. The churches and their respective leaders are largely in the dark, suffering from theological inertia and spiritual myopia. Mention of the Basileia confuses some and amuses others; many wonder why we invoke a concept and an idea that, really, does not belong to ecclesiastical parlance.

A great deal of the confusion and unease relates to the fact that the Basileia is very much more about spirituality than religion. The desire to relate lovingly and justly is a universal human aspiration, the exploration and expression of which connects me to the inner spiritual core of my being. The search for meaning, as I strive to relate more authentically, can never be explained solely on the basis of psychology or anthropology. Deeper voices cry out for recognition; deeper yearnings begin to unfold. Mystery wriggles its way through the intricacies of wonder and confusion. Experience intensifies; the heat of passion, the warmth of emotion, the fire that threatens to consume, all come into the playfulness of the divine delirium.

Mythologists like Joseph Campbell (1985), James Hillman (1985), Carol S. Pearson (1989), Jean Shinoda Boelen (1984, 1989) help us to unravel these experiences by drawing on the primordial example of ancient Greek gods and goddesses. As already noted, Thomas Moore (1982, 1984) does this in a particularly poignant way in his attempts to recover soul as a central notion in contemporary spirituality. The 'mythological' approach is particularly helpful for those whose spiritual journey leads them into counselling or psychotherapy; whose spiritual exploration has brought them into contact with the esoteric world of 'new age' consciousness, or those who have become so disillusioned with formal religion that they have been inspired to follow some different, alternative way to uncovering their spiritual vision.

Valid though it is for huge numbers of people, the 'mythological' approach leaves largely untouched the millions who starve for spiritual nourishment, particularly the billions who are marginalised because of hunger, poverty, dislocation, oppression, warfare, injustice, exploitation, etc. These are the people to which the Jesus message is relevant in a unique way; from a Kingdom perspective one cannot be a Christian without giving priority to the poor and deprived of our world.

To engage authentically with the Basileia, to be converted to live out of its meaning and challenge, we must hear its summons to us in the lives and witness of the poor of the Earth. From the perspective of the Basileia, it is not primarily a question of improving the lot of the poor – that can so easily become another masquerade for patriarchal manipulation; rather our hearts must become transparent to the cry from the poor for a more just, equitable and loving world. Until and unless we can expose ourselves to that paradoxical experience, we may never grow into the receptive, listening, caring and vulnerable people who can encounter the living face of God in those closest to God's heart.

One of the most shocking statements in the Gospels is Christ's own affirmation of the poor, the sinners and the outcasts, as the first to enter God's New Reign, as the ones who will point the way to the rest of us. Try as we like to rationalise, domesticate or theologise about it, that message remains unambiguous, a thorn in the side for all who try to follow the Christian way, complete nonsense to the patriarchs of our age and of every age. It is in our trans-patriarchal state – of vulnerability and transparency to paradox and mystery – that we can begin to rediscover the call of the Christian Basileia and in that way begin to appreciate the radically new vision of Jesus of Nazareth.

A spirituality of the Basileia must never be reduced to the strategy or theology of any one church or religious system, nor indeed to the vision of all the churches and religions put together. The Basileia is about radical transformation for authentic human and planetary life. Its ideal and target is clear; its strategy is what baffles people, particularly those among us formed in linear logic, rational thought and patriarchal structure.

The Basileia thrives on the paradoxical: the last first and the first last; it proffers an upside-down world; it ridicules the rich and the powerful and all those who claim the Earth as their own; it summons the weak and the oppressed to a joy and freedom that look crazy to the 'powers that be'; it adulterates all our self-made gods (especially those of formal religion) for the God of surprises, the God of raging justice, the God of passionate love, the God who becomes so radically human that it seems ridiculous to those in our world who are spiritually alienated on the one hand, or saturated in religiosity on the other.

The spirituality being invoked is not really new; in fact, it is very old. First, it requires us to take fully to heart – and with all the joyful seriousness we can muster – the reality of being human. Second, we are called to realise that new way of being human, not in the competitive isolation that belongs to the patriarchal age of 'divide and conquer', but in the inclusive realm of the whole of creation, without which our human lives have little or no meaning. Third, it validates our deepest aspirations to live in harmony with mystery and with the divine within and without. Fourth, it seeks to integrate the shadow – the poor that are always with us, the rejected one on the side of the road – and through the encounter with darkness, journey towards the light that liberates. Fifth, it calls us to be in interdependent communion, because only in the reworking of our relationships, over and over again, will we continue to rediscover, not once, but several times, our true selves. Finally, it challenges us to transcend our fabricated religious systems so that we can engage more dynamically with our co-creative God in bringing about 'a new heaven and a new earth'.

Reclaiming our incarnational humanity

The spirituality of the Basileia calls to judgment and accountability every value system, religious and otherwise. Although primarily focused on the humanum, its uniqueness and sacredness, it never advocates an anthropocentrism that seeks to lord it over the rest of creation. The ethics of the Basileia are all about the conditions that make for right relationships, with every life-form, planet Earth and the cosmos included.

There is nothing in the Christian Gospel that justifies humans in standing over against creation as masters or lords, nor is there anything to validate a group of humans in either the political or ecclesiastical realm to claim access to a special form of divine wisdom. The Emmanuel (God with us) of the Christian Gospel is God totally and unashamedly immersed in creation, with all its light and shadow. Only by that same immersion in the world of daily life can we hope to encounter that co-creative God. That encounter becomes the ultimate relationship in the light of which all others begin to make sense, and without which we are condemned to anomie and ennui all the days of our lives.

When we take the Basileia as our starting point in exploring the Christian understanding of the spiritual journey, we are invited to let go of many traditional notions which portray the Christian faith in an exclusive and imperialistic fashion.

There is a quality of humanity and humility (from *humus*, meaning earth) in the Christian Gospel which is truly unique and yet belongs to all peoples of all times and places. Our Christian uniqueness is the very gift we receive from all others and offer back in return. It is not something to be hoarded and converted into a patriarchal, imperialistic ideology to lord it over others. It is in our mutual inter-relatedness that we discover, time and again, our true identity.

The vision of the Basileia opens up new worlds of possibility and hope, a strategy to make real and vibrant the relationships that augment life and diminish the forces of destruction and despair. When we reduce the Basileia to an explicit religious context, then we run the risk of subjecting it to ecclesiastical control (by equating Kingdom with church) or we equate it with a utopian state that can only be attained in the life hereafter. In both cases, we miss the prophetic jolt of having to engage with the transformative present under the impetus and challenge of the transfigured future.

It has taken us some 2,000 years to catch up on the paradigm shift of the New Reign of God as inaugurated in the person and life of Jesus. That shift pre-empts and prefigures the dissolution of the patriarchal world-view with its dominant wisdom of divide-and-conquer. More importantly, it proffers a new praxis of relational interdependence, including not merely the human, but the planetary and cosmic dimensions as well. Nothing short of that global vision will enable humanity to cross the threshold into the new age that is, and has been, dawning upon our world for the past 2,000 years.

For many people, 2,000 years is a time-span they can scarcely comprehend. Our linear, rational, and cerebral formation has left us with deranged minds and suffocated imaginations. Not only are we alienated culturally, but we are also cut off historically. The sacrament of the present moment can be an impressive veneer for a great deal of sacrilegious navel-gazing. What we need above all else is a spiritual vision that will enable us to reclaim the divine-human co-creativity that has impregnated our evolution over millions of years and is synthesised evocatively in the vision of the New Reign of God.

Some begin to despair when they realise that it has taken us

2,000 years to grasp the full impact of the Jesus vision. If we follow the view that civilisation has only been with us for some 5,000 years, then, indeed, we have good reason for despondency and hopelessness. But when we stretch our visual and imaginative horizons to incorporate and appropriate our evolutionary story – and that of our planet and cosmos – and we can develop a spirituality that enables us to see the creative power of God at work in all that, then we come home to our true selves as creatures that belong to a great cosmic story spanning millions and billions of years. Within that time-span, 2,000 years is a mere second, for which we can humbly and justifiably forgive ourselves for our patriarchal rebelliousness, and now have the humility and courage to leave all that behind for the new vision that beckons us forth.

The Basileia, from a Christian viewpoint, serves as an encapsulation of divine–human co-creativity, spanning the millennia of evolutionary unfolding. As noted earlier, the Basileia is very much about expanded horizons towards greater inclusiveness and egalitarianism. For Christians, a vision of the Kingdom that fails to stretch us – humanly, spiritually and culturally – cannot possibly be the authentic one. A spirituality of the Kingdom, at all times, opens us up to the entire universe, to behold the glory and grandeur of our co-creative God, spearheading the creation and destruction of our evolutionary coming-to-be.

As we move into the trans-patriarchal era, we realise that the more we open up to the grandeur without, the more we must learn anew to reconnect within. Above everything else, the Basileia is about the ability to engage, contemplatively and creatively, in the right relationships that will beget a new world order, characterised by justice, love, peace and liberation for all. To that end we are invited to commit all our energy, all our wisdom, and all our love!

On grounding the new vision

Home is where one starts from. As we grow older
The world becomes stranger, the pattern more complicated.
We must be still and still moving,
Into another intensity;
For a further union, a deeper communion.

T. S. Eliot

Ritual is neither a detached contemplation of the world nor a passive sym-
bolization of it but is the performance of an act in which people confront
one kind of power with another, and rehearse their own future. . . . Ritual
ought not be defined by any particular beliefs with which it may be associated, for ritual is prior to belief.

Tom F. Driver

THROUGHOUT THE AGES spirituality has been associated
with a particular set of convictions and values, embraced
within a particular lifestyle and celebrated regularly in devotion,
prayer, ritual or worship. A Christian spirituality is based on those
values and virtues which are highly prized in the Christian Gospels:
love, compassion, service, justice, right relationships and suffering
in the cause of right, a central statement of which are the Beatitudes
(Matt. 5:1–12). How these values are to be appropriated and lived
out has been the subject of the church's teachings and laws down
through the ages. Finally, the Christian church also provides a
repertoire of prayers (personal and communal) and a sacramental
system, to enable Christians to engage more meaningfully in the
central experiences of personal and planetary life.

Hinduism, Buddhism, Islam – each of the religions has evolved
a similar tripartite system around central beliefs, congruent behaviours and a ritual repertoire for prayer and worship. Over the
centuries, a subtle and at times quite overt competition arose
between the different religions, each giving priority and superiority to its vision and praxis. In recent decades, however, a growing

coming-together – in dialogue and mutual engagement – has been evidenced, especially in Christian cultures.

The reader can readily see that religion and spirituality mean essentially the same thing in the above outline. As a Christian phenomenon, spirituality has been viewed with suspicion and anxiety. For much of the Christian era it was relegated to the closed sphere of monastic seclusion or subsequently, to the post-Renaissance environment of the university where it became a sub-set of philosophical debate and logical argumentation. In the seventeenth century, spirituality referred exclusively to the interior life of Christians, often expressed in bizarre devotional practices. By the eighteenth century, it refers to the perfection associated with mystical states, unattainable by the majority of ordinary people. Finally, in the eighteenth and nineteenth centuries, academic status was granted to the study of the spiritual life, but only in the context of ethics or moral theology.

In every age, the meaning and impact of spirituality has been influenced by factors of global proportion. To understand the emerging spirituality we need to be aware of the global ferment of our time: a growing awareness of our planet as one Earth, destined to be shared equally by all; unprecedented scientific discoveries such as the quantum theory of the 1920s (the theological implications of which I explore in Ó Murchú, 1997); the growing realisation that nothing in our world – religious or otherwise – can be comprehensively understood apart from a multi-disciplinary mode of exploration; the captivating mystical visions of astronauts from outer space confirming our unity-within-diversity in what seems to be an alive planet Earth; finally, the nauseating disgust that after centuries of religious fervour, moralising and proselytising, we are left with a world divided, lacerated and desecrated by pain, inequality, barbarity and warfare, much of which is fuelled by religious bigotry.

It is these and the many other changes referred to throughout the pages of this book that have birthed the sense (perhaps even the science) of the new spirituality. It is a spirituality that belongs to the world and its peoples and not to some distant God in heaven or to an ultimate state of nirvana. It is a spirituality that transcends what each and all the religions claim to represent. It is a spirituality that engages with the search for meaning as people struggle to inter-relate more authentically in what we progressively consider to be an interdependent world, within an eternally evolving universe. It is a spirituality that invites us to break out of all our anthropocentric enclaves – religious and political – and reclaim the whole of creation as our one true home.

Throughout the pages of this book, I outline some of the significant departures for those who feel called to embrace the new spirituality, the many trappings, expectations and institutions that we will need to outgrow and leave behind. More importantly, I try to describe the novel landscape, with its as yet largely untrod pathways, this virgin territory that requires our courageous, creative and risky involvement. In this chapter, I wish to offer some pointers on what might be the corresponding namings to the values, behaviours and rituals so long associated with the culture of formal religion.

We are creatures of value

The anthropologist, Mircea Eliade, and the psychologist, C. G. Jung both claim that all values are based on innate universal aspirations which people aspire towards and yearn for throughout the whole of time and culture. These archetypal values are foundational to all human yearning, and include such simple and significant ones as unadulterated love, truth, honesty, integrity, peace, liberty and the creative complementarity of the Yin and the Yang. All the world religions seek to enculturate these values and offer guidelines for their appropriation and integration in various cultural and geographical settings.

Consequently, in the deep story of each religion, we encounter a value-oriented vision upon which the dogmas and institutions of that religion are constructed. The example I offer (in Chapter 10) is the Christian notion of the Basileia (the New Reign of God), with its underlying archetypal values of justice, love, peace and liberation. At this primordial level, Christians connect with the universal sense of spirituality which underpins all religion. Spirituality is older, more enduring and more pervasive than all the religions put together. Spirituality, therefore, engages with the core values, with the foundational value-orientation which belongs to the mutual co-existence of person and planet alike. The values that the religions claim to foster and safeguard – often in the exclusive context of a specific religion, or denomination – belong essentially and primarily to spirituality. Religion is the name we give to the enculturation of such values in the patriarchal culture of the past 8,000–10,000 years.

Not all the values perpetuated in the name of formal religion are congruent with spiritual unfolding. As indicated earlier in this book, we now understand formal religion to be very much the product – indeed, the icing on the cake – of the patriarchal culture of post-Agriculture/Revolution times. The prevailing culture was unambiguously a dominator one (see Eisler, 1987; Gimbutas, 1991), with the values of divide-and-conquer predominating over all other aspirations. The oppressive end result is all too familiar: market-competition where the poor and weak always lose out; power-acquisition, often reaching compulsive levels; land exploitation, female subjugation, feminine suppression, anthropocentricising the divine (i.e. creating God figures in the image of the patriarchal male). These are clearly not the values of the New Reign of God depicted in the Christian Gospels, nor indeed do they even remotely resemble the deep values upheld by other world religions.

And this brings us once again to what may well be the most controversial and daunting claim of the new spirituality: religion is a temporary reality that in all probability has outlived its usefulness. Spiritual engagement for our time is not about revitalising or renewing religion and its accompanying moral, dogmatic and liturgical practices. Rather, the primary task of spirituality is to enable and empower people to reclaim the fundamental *raison d'être* of all religion: the engagement with, and practical living out of, those deep values which alone can assuage the spiritual hunger in the heart of every human being.

How to enculturate key values is one of the most urgent questions facing our planetary and personal civilisation today. The notion that we live in a value-free or value-less society is one of the many deceptive and convoluted dogmas engineered by the dominator culture. Value orientation is implanted in the deepest recesses of our beings as human creatures, and in the very fabric of creation itself as a living, evolutionary organism. We cannot avoid being people of value; everything we think, say and do is impregnated with value. Even the argument for a value-free culture is itself a statement of value.

Not all value is necessarily good and precisely because of the archetypal and primal nature of value orientation, the impact of light and shadow is always at work. Ultimately all values are geared to the wholeness of life promised in all the great religions, but our attempts to aspire towards and attain that wholeness are often affected by greed, selfishness, exploitation and power-seeking. The person who robs and murders is doing an evil act – not for the sake of evil – but for a perceived good. In a world of so much outrageous suffering and injustice, this statement can feel like a banality that enrages and disgusts the hearer, but it is a conviction of spirituality that we must retain and continually strive to appropriate.

The human will-to-meaning may become grossly distorted and convoluted, but the ultimate goal of that will is always the good. No matter how depraved the human condition becomes, there is always – sometimes buried under layers of disfunctionality – a spiritual affirmation of life. This is more readily understood if we try to out-grow the age-old Christian conviction that there exists in human beings a radical, innate deformity, popularly known as original sin, always de-railing the potential to do good. Beyond the personal sin however, is the structural (or systemic) sin, which is what often makes it so difficult to pursue the fundamental goodness that lies at the heart of all individual beings.

The most destructive force for evil is systemic rather than personal; oppressive and destructive systems are what drive many people to behave in immoral and destructive ways. To become more value-centred people, not only must persons change, but also many of the structures that surround us, including the religious ones.

Holistic ways of behaving

To appropriate and enculturate spiritual values, a number of pre-conditions have been named by several contemporary researchers and these highlight some of the behaviour changes we will need to bring about in earthing the vision of the new spirituality. Essentially this means learning afresh to relate in a holistic and interconnected way, as we strive to transcend our competitive will-to-power.

1. The need to abandon our mechanistic modelling is long overdue; it fuels a power for oppression and destruction that is no longer tenable. We need to move toward more holistic ways of engaging with our world.
2. We must learn afresh how to befriend the entire creation, but

particularly our planetary home, the Earth. We need to shed the remnants of religious ambivalence towards, or rejection of, the Earth and move toward more caring and sustainable ways of living, which is a moral imperative for our time.

3. We need to transcend rational values of the head in favour of feminine approaches of the heart.

4. We need a new concerted global effort to break down the rigid divisions that culminate in nation states, independent religions, vying tribes and competing races. Partnership and not separation is the crucial spiritual value for our future.

5. Prizing competition as a primary value is a sure pathway to species catastrophe, possibly total annihilation. Co-operation is an essential value to guarantee a more sustainable and spiritually radiant future.

Consequently, the moral and ethical codes drawn up to further the new spirituality will need to embody global, inclusive, co-operative, egalitarian and feminine values, requiring quite new strategies based primarily on dialogue, mutual interaction, empowerment of the many creatures excluded by the contemporary impoverishment of body, mind and spirit, and courageous new ways to dissolve the dualistic separation of the political and the spiritual spheres of life.

In ethical terms our greatest challenge is to abandon our individually based personal morality in favour of a more planet-related ethical system. Juxtaposing person and planet is the root cause of so much of our sin and suffering. Setting humanity over, or against, the material creation is an anthropocentric ploy validated by all the formal religions. It is alien and alienating for millions of people in today's world; it is incongruous with the emerging story of the new cosmology (Chapter 6) and undermines the spiritual hunger for a more humane and God-centred global civilisation.

If we wish to create for ourselves a future of greater meaning and integrity, we must learn to behave and relate more interdependently. We must refrain from raping the womb of Mother Earth on which we are dependent for everything that nourishes and sustains us. We must destruct – and then reconstruct – the political, economic and religious systems which currently perpetuate an ideology of ruthless exploitation, oppressive domination and the savage destruction of life at several different levels.

Before we ever hope to create this new moral agenda, we will need to challenge and affirm one another on the need to do so. One step towards the creation of that more enlightened state is the recreation of meaningful rituals that will engage more deeply our hearts and imaginations. This third element may prove to be the most crucial of all.

Reawakening the power of ritual

Our Western culture suffers from a conspicuous lack of relevant and meaningful ritual. As creatures of meaning we need spaces (and places) in which to narrate our stories in a way that will help us to negotiate the search for meaning. And if those stories are to percolate into our culture we need social occasions in which to formalise – in word and symbol – the yearnings and aspirations inherent in those stories.

Our faith traditions are intended to provide us with such ritual outlets – sometimes referred to as ceremonies, liturgies or sacraments. But in nearly all cases the inherited tradition of ritual is overloaded with archaic and outdated symbols, gestures and language; these elements belong primarily to the culture of bygone days and fail to awaken a sense of the numinous in our contemporary consciousness.

Furthermore, many of the sacraments have been ritually abused by the very people who sought to propagate their sacred meaning. In the Catholic tradition, the Mass has become a formalised gathering, attendance at which is obligatory under pain of sin. The sacrament of penance (Confession), intended to mediate an experience of healing and forgiveness by a God of unconditional love, has been used over the centuries to inculcate guilt, fear and subservience to 'legitimate' power. The Catholic system (rather than individual people or clergy) has used sacramental practice to intimidate the faithful into subjugation and to justify religious patriarchy in its voracious hunger for power and control.

In creating new rituals for the new spirituality, we can draw on both the old and the new. Many of the great religions are rediscovering the communitarian nature of sacramental tradition and experience (see Driver, 1991, ch. 8). Thus, Donovan (1989) seeks to reclaim the richness of daily sacramentality, especially through people's time-honoured traditions of communal interaction. In the case of the Eucharist (Mass), therefore, we need to relearn a great deal about the sacred dimensions of our daily food which many people first experience by sharing family meals. Confession needs to focus more directly and explicitly on people's felt needs for reconciliation and the healing of hurts and misunderstandings that arise in daily experience. Serious commitments, whether short- or long-term, need to be ritualised and celebrated within the community, or communities, that inculcated the desire for relationship in the first place; celebrating a marriage in a temple, church or registry office often distracts from the communal significance of the experience and diminishes the challenge to the community to support and nourish this new partnership just as it contributed to its formation in the first place.

Revamping and readapting well-tested models from bygone days is a reasonable suggestion to which many people will warm. However, we have to acknowledge and affirm the desire of many spiritual seekers of our time for a radically new repertoire of ritual expression. This, in part, arises because the spiritual upsurge today includes many people of no particular religious tradition, others of the tradition whose experience has not been life-giving or enriching, and still others who feel that the old systems have become so congealed and outdated that they cannot be revitalised in a way that would speak to contemporary experience.

For proponents of mainstream religion, questions of continuity and discontinuity surface at this juncture. There are those who claim that authentic ritual or sacramental expression needs to arise out of a former tradition and faithfully imbibe fundamental, unchanging meanings. This is a well-intentioned argument, but frequently betraying a rational Western mind-set that often thrives on an imperialism of continuity that entitles some to impose on others Western forms and structures, thus savagely undermining the sacred traditions of other peoples and places. The destructive aftermath is all too obvious in Africa and South America as we read about the triumph and barbarity of several European missionaries.

Those who argue for continuity in ritualistic expression are stating a deep truth insofar as peoples of all ages and cultures tend to ritualise key human and planetary experiences such as birth, death, transitional experiences (becoming an adult), commitments (as in marriage), seasonal changes, the new moon, and a range of rituals to avert the threats of impending danger. However, a hugely diverse set of ritual expressions accompany the celebration of these special occasions. Moreover, there are cultural differences in how these events are celebrated, often undermined by proponents of formal religion who tend to impose a universal sameness on all their rites and ceremonies.

Rituals for our time

Before reviewing some dominant ritual expressions for today's world and its peoples it would be a serious omission not to highlight the revival of the practice of meditation in recent decades. What in the early part of this century was considered to be the reserve of those specially dedicated to God in monasteries and convents, has now been reclaimed as a divine endowment bequeathed to all humans.

The desire for, and capacity to meditate – that is to become quiet and centred around an inner core of meaning – is a gift bestowed upon every human being. It is a dimension of the divine seed sown in the heart of each person, awakening a desire to be centred, realigned to the fundamental mystery of existence, at peace with reality, a sense of home-coming to one's true self. Whether pursued in an Eastern or Western form, against a Christian or Buddhist background, is of relative importance. This is a wisdom and a propensity that cannot, and should not, be reduced to the dictates of any one, or even all the formal religions.

Although meditation is an innate, God-given propensity, it does require gentle and enlightened tutoring. It is a powerful medium of inner growth which awakens forces of light and darkness. It can easily become a self-delusory and self-destructive ego-trip. In learning to meditate, we need the guidance of experienced, centred teachers, people who themselves are immersed in the practice (and not just in the tradition – although that, too, is helpful) of what they are seeking to share and communicate. Many of the outstanding guides of our time, people like J. Krishnamurti, Ram Dass, Shunryn Suzuki Roshi, Kalu Rinpoche and Thich Nhat Hanh (see Kornfield, 1993), belong to the great Eastern faith traditions where the practice of meditation carries a sacred history thousands of years old, long pre-dating the emergence of formal religions.[10]

For many spiritual seekers of our time, the most meaningful prayer or ritual experience is a space for centring prayer or meditation, done in the presence of a group on a regular basis. The frequency tends to be once a week, on the understanding that the person meditates on one's own at least once a day. The group dimension seems to create a coherence and affirmation of the integration within, and the harmony without, which seem to be the primary achievements of this ancient practice.

Most people, however, also imbibe a need for some form of symbolic engagement, around significant experiences, typified in ancient cultures by Rites of Passage, and in mainstream religions by devotions, ceremonies or sacraments. Many of these rites are devised to celebrate transitional moments such as birth, death, coming of age (puberty), becoming an adult, etc. Many of those rituals have become excessively institutionalised and largely lost their capacity to evoke or awaken meaning and integration, e.g. the sacrament of Confirmation in the Catholic tradition intended to mark entry into young adulthood, but has become a largely empty ritual seeking to foment church allegiance.

In contemporary human experience, there are many key moments in personal life that need to be celebrated ritually, e.g. sexual maturity in early adolescence; entry and termination of significant relationships; college graduation; first day at work; movement to a first (or a new) home; female menopause; various healing rituals for sickness, loss and bereavement; retirement; death.

The context of such celebrations is also important. A religious ambience in itself does not guarantee meaningful ritual, because often the religious context undermines or seems to supersede the significant cultural dimensions. Many religious rituals focus on the individual person in his/her unique self; increasingly, we are acknowledging the communal (familial) context that is uniquely significant for that person; as yet, we give scant attention to the planetary context that impinges upon that person and upon his/her local community. This latter dimension is the one that has been seriously undermined by religious ceremonies, where the Earth-basis of elements like water, oil, light, incense, bread, wine, etc. tends to be totally overlooked.

At a communal level, we engage in a vast range of ritual behaviours many of which have been absorbed into our daily living and hence have largely lost their unique spiritual significance, e.g. birthdays, weddings, funerals, parties for various occasions, carnivals, parades, national days of celebration. But we seriously lack rituals to engage creatively with conflict (locally or globally), political relations, global distribution of the Earth's resources, etc.

Some contemporary writers (e.g. Driver, 1991; Some, 1993) attribute the rise in reckless violence to the fact that we are a ritually deprived people. We do not have meaningful outlets to ventilate deep feelings, whether positive or negative, nor can we channel in a meaningful way those negative feelings that otherwise lead to destructive projecting onto other people or onto the environment. There is an instinctive safeguard built into a great deal of animal behaviour, whereby creatures of the same species transform heightened emotions (e.g. aggression) into ritual play and resolve what otherwise could become a dangerous digression. We humans, being creatures of freedom and creativity, must develop these rituals for ourselves; without them we remain humanly and spiritually depraved, threatening not merely our own equilibrium but the peace and harmony of the entire world order.

Work as ritual

Fox (1994) writes at some length about the relationship of ritual and work. He concurs with other theorists (Handy, 1994; Henderson, 1981; Robertson, 1986) that the traditional role of work as a primary means to earn a wage no longer makes cultural nor economic sense; consequently, we need to reinvent the role and meaning of work in our lives. In this way, work itself, no longer constrained by the consumerist compulsion of wage-earning, can assume ritual significance of immense personal and cultural import.

Our work can be a real celebration of our gifts and talents, offered to other people and to creation, in a joyful, play-filled and 'prayerful' interaction with our world. The desacralising of work – which contributes to so much boredom, competition and so much unresolved conflict in workplaces – can be reversed as we reclaim a sense of work as our mutual planetary contribution to creating a better world for all creatures. In this way, human work more readily assumes a spiritual significance and we begin to perceive ourselves anew as co-creative creatures co-operating with our co-creative God.

In rediscovering the sacredness of work, we can release once more the unique creative resources of poets, artists, sculptors, musicians, dancers, symbol-makers, those subversively prophetic people marginalised by the formal economy, because they threaten the regimentation so necessary for that system to survive. A culture that chooses to release and befriend the power of the artist becomes much more transparent to the creative and transformative power of ritual. A culture that chooses to unlock the slavery and drudgery of the 'factory' and reclaim the right and duty of every person for meaningful work can scarcely avoid the discovery that all work is sacred, not just because it contributes to the divine unfolding of creation, but, because of its very nature, it releases the divine energy from within people themselves.

Currently, we are slaves to work precisely because we have enslaved our work, mechanised it for anthropocentric gain and earthly exploitation. As Fox and others rightly suggest, the reinvention of work is a central element in the spiritual revolution of our time, a spontaneous catalyst for the revitalisation of ritual, of a quality and design that will engage the contemporary spiritual seekers.

As indicated in Chapter 7, those who develop and foster the new feminist consciousness contribute courageously and creatively to new ritual expression (cf. Ruether, 1985; Walker, 1990). Because some such rituals, e.g. women celebrating their own Eucharist, disregard the official procedures of church and religion, they are often portrayed not merely as subversive and misleading, but as being 'magical' and 'pagan' and, consequently, a threat to personal well-being as well as to religious orthodoxy. In fact, my experience of women's self-created rituals indicates a great deal of sensitivity, wisdom and integrity. Some will express rage, anger and strong denunciation of formal religious expectations but, in my opinion, never more vociferously than Jesus did when confronted with the religious norms and institutions of his time.

The feminist contribution to the revitalisation of ritual, strikes me as being prophetically motivated and activated with a great deal of sensitivity, creativity and imagination. It deserves to be considered as a primary source of animation in this urgent spiritual and cultural task.

Feminist rituals often draw on ancient and modern Rites of Passage to underpin contemporary expressions. Our Christian tradition tends to be dismissive and largely ignorant of such rites, often attributing them to the 'pre-religious', unenlightened minds of uncultured pagan peoples. This is a gross and unjust

misrepresentation of very ancient and sacred customs which pre-
date, and often provide a more developed enculturation of formal
religious rites or sacraments. Such rites deserve a much more
informed and respectful understanding which, I believe, would
provide us with a solid and authentic foundation for the revitalised
rituals of our culture and its peoples so urgently needed at this
time.

Rediscovering ritual space

The ritual hunger I write about in this chapter may be described as
a type of ferment seeping into the consciousness of many people
and beginning to take shape in a vast range of expression and form.
For the greater part, it is an underground movement, sometimes
fearful of the denunciation it might evoke from the formal religious
institutions; other times, provocatively counter-cultural, determined to sever all links or association with formal religion. Thus
far, there seems little scope for dialogue; the old and the new are
unlikely to meet or interact.

This is a disturbing state of play for those concerned about continuity and some preservation of sacred tradition. It seems to me
that the tradition is not under threat, because as indicated previously, the revitalisation often implies the retrieval of long-lost
wisdom, and this will contribute to the growth of the tradition
without which it cannot continue. My concern is for the millions
who are no longer nourished by the 'old' – the thousands who every
year abandon formal religion and its practice – a trend which in all
probability will become even more pronounced in the twenty-first
century – and end up in a spiritual wasteland. These people abandon the old because it no longer nourishes them; but because the
alternative ritual outlets are largely 'underground' the disillusioned
are unaware of their existence, ill-informed on their meaning and
significance, or fearful that they might end up in another dead end.
Instead, they opt for the 'safe' world of post-modernism, but as
indicated in the Introduction, this is effectively a world devoid of
meaning where dualistic fantasies feed on a rhetoric that explains
away, rather than explains, the unfolding world of our time.

The spiritual wasteland is a dead end, and for many in the Western world culminates in the ultimate act of abandonment: suicide
or, alternatively, in a life half lived, sustained by stimulants or anti-

depressants to retain a semblance of sanity. Even common sense indicates that people cannot tolerate this meaninglessness for long and the decision to re-emerge is of its very nature a re-awakening of spiritual desire.

What to do with those awakening feelings, how to talk about them, where and with whom to explore them are among the perennial questions of our time – urgent, not just for a meaningful spirituality of the future, but indeed for the survival of civilisation itself. All indications are that the wisdom provided by formal religious institutions and those who represent them, is of little use in addressing these burning contemporary issues. We need new ways of befriending, supporting and enlightening each other in this new exploration and, in due course, we'll need new rituals to acknowledge, negotiate and celebrate the spiritual revolution that is waiting to irrupt onto the world stage. Its irruption will be a timely event – not without its chaos and confusion – and blessed are those who are open to receive it. It may well prove to be the greatest surprise of the twenty-first century.

Notes

1. Being a non-theistic belief-system, it is debatable whether or not one should describe Buddhism as a formal religion. In the context of this book, it merits special attention since its promotion of meditation, mindfulness and compassion evokes universal sympathy, particularly from those seeking fresh spiritual meaning in today's world.

2. In a similar vein, I'd like to draw the reader's attention to the work of Ninian Smart and Steven Constantine, *Christian Systematic Theology in a World Context,* HarperCollins, 1991.

    The descriptive adjective, trans-Christian is used throughout the book, never pre-Christian or post-Christian.

3. Contrary to many contemporary works, feminist and otherwise, I use the term 'patriarchy' in a specific historical and cultural context. I trace its origins to the rise of the Agricultural Revolution around 8000 BCE. Across the humanly populated world of the time, people (men particularly) sought to bring the forces of nature directly under human control. Land was objectified as an instrument of production, and the more you had, the more you could produce. To obtain maximum benefits from the soil, all 'wild' forces were tamed; even humans themselves had to submit to those who chose to dictate the terms of domination, division and control. Planet Earth was fragmented and divided into what we now know as nation states and ethnic groups; thus were sown the seeds of warfare!

    The masculine will-to-power, the insatiable urge to divide and conquer, became the over-riding principle of the age of patriarchy and has prevailed to our own time. Currently, there are many indications that the patriarchal value-system is crumbling and is in a state of irreversible disintegration.

4. Many people warm to this principle since it validates the view that everything is geared to the evolution of an intelligent life-form like our own. However, it also embodies strong anthropomorphic overtones veering towards the view that the universe would be fundamentally unintelligible if we had not the intelligence to interpret what's going on there. All of which comes dangerously close to asserting that we, humans, are the ultimate species above and beyond which there is only God and eternal existence – an exalted status that entitles us to act like 'God' in our governance of creation. For the scientific exposition, see John D. Barrow & Frank F. Tippler, *The Anthropic Cosmological Principle,* Oxford University Press, 1986.

5. Some readers will be familiar with the Enneagram, a Sufi-based personality profile which uses the three categories of head, heart and gut: head refers to

people in whom cerebral, thinking processes dominate; heart are those for whom feelings are highly significant, and gut is used to describe people whose visceral instincts dictate their behaviour and responses (the gutsy type). It is important to note that psychological and spiritual growth requires a balanced integration of all three elements.

6. Guthrie (1993, p. 6) uses the related term 'anthropomorphism' described as '. . . attributing human characteristics to non-human phenomena. . . . Faced with uncertainty, we bet on the most significant possibility.' In other words, we are brainwashed into putting ourselves first – at all times and in all situations – driven by the delusion that this will augment our survival and progress as a species.

7. While I do not wish to underestimate the psycho-sexual influences surfacing from the personal unconscious (in the Freudian sense), my use of the term, in the present context, follows the Jungian approach and Jung's understanding of the Collective Unconscious. The upsurge of psycho-sexual creativity in our world today cannot be explained solely in personal or inter-personal terms, consciously or unconsciously. Driving forces of a more cultural and etheric nature seem to be at work and these are best understood, I suggest, by employing Jung's concept of the Collective Unconscious. Some relevant information in Frederica R. Halligan & John J. Shea (eds), *The Fires of Desire*, New York: Crossroad, 1993.

8. Monick (1987) provides a largely positive analysis of the phallus as a symbol for assertive and creative sexual power in men; this view needs to be complemented with the equally insightful presentation of Wyly (1989) whose primary concern is the shadow energy with priapism, masculine inflation and ego aggrandisement among its commonly destructive projections.

9. The claim that there are strong links between repressed male sexuality and the culture of modern warfare is powerfully illustrated by Morgan (1989), who also highlights the sexualised nature of behaviour and training in contemporary military culture.

10. We in the West need to be wary and suspicious of Eastern movements that couch the passing on of their wisdom in Western commercial and consumerist terms. The Transcendental Meditation (TM) Movement, based on a very ancient and sacred wisdom, has, unfortunately, fallen into this trap.

Bibliography

Abraham, Ralph (1994), *Chaos, Gaia, Eros*, San Francisco: HarperSanFrancisco.

Baring, Anne & Cashford, Jules (1991), *The Myth of the Goddess*, London & New York: Viking Arkana.

Barnes, Michael (1984), *In the Presence of Mystery: An Introduction to the Story of Human Religiousness*, Mystic (Conn.): Twenty-Third Publications.

Berry, Thomas (1988), *The Dream of the Earth*, San Francisco: Sierra Club Books.

Bertens, Hans (1995), *The Idea of the Postmodern: A History*, London & New York: Routledge.

Boelen, Jean Shinoda (1984), *Goddess in Everywoman*, San Francisco: Harper & Row. (1989), *Gods in Everyman*, San Francisco: Harper & Row.

Brock, Rita Nakashima (1992), *Journeys By Heart*, New York: Crossroad.

Brown, Peter (1990), *The Body and Society: Men, Women and Sexual Renunciation in Early Christianity*, London and Boston: Faber & Faber.

Brueggemann, Walter (1978), *The Prophetic Imagination*, Philadelphia: Fortress Press. (1986), *The Hopeful Imagination*, Philadelphia: Fortress Press.

Bullough, Vern L. (1976), *Sexual Variance in Society and History*, New York: John Wiley & Sons.

Burrows, B., Mayne, A. & Newbury, P. (1991), *Into the 21st Century*, London: Adamantine Press.

Campbell, Joseph (1985), *Myths to Live By*, London: Paladin Books.

Capra, Fritjof (1982), *The Turning Point*, New York: Simon & Schuster.

Carr, Anne E. (1988), *Transforming Grace: Christian Tradition and Woman's Experience*, San Francisco: Harper & Row.

Childe, V. Gordan (1958), *The Dawn of European Civilization*, New York: Alfred Knopf.

Chittister, Joan (1995), *The Fire in These Ashes*, Kansas City: Sheed & Ward.

Chopp, Rebecca (1986), *The Praxis of Suffering*, Maryknoll, NY: Orbis Books. (1989), *The Power to Speak: Feminism, Language, God*, New York: Crossroad.

Collins, Paul (1995), *God's Earth: Religion as if Matter Really Mattered*, Melbourne: HarperCollins; Dublin: Gill & Macmillan

Conlon, James (1990), *Geo-Justice: A Preferential Option for the Earth*, San Jose, CA: Resource Publications Inc.

Daly, Gabriel (1988), *Creation and Redemption*, Dublin: Gill & Macmillan; Wilmington DE: Michael Glazier.

Daly, Mary (1973), *Beyond God the Father*, Boston: Beacon Press. (New edition, 1985). (1978), *Gyn/Ecology*, Boston: Beacon Press.

Davidson, John (1989), *The Secret of the Creative Vacuum*, London: C.W. Daniel.

Davies, Paul (1992), *The Mind of God*, New York: Simon & Schuster.

de Chardin, Teilhard (1970), *The Phenomenon of Man*, London: Fontana.

Denaux, Adelbert (1996), 'Did Jesus Found the Church', *Louvain Studies*, Vol. 21, pp. 25–45.

Donovan, Vincent J. (1989), *The Church in the Midst of Creation*, Maryknoll, NY: Orbis Books.

Driver, Tom F.(1991), *The Magic of Ritual*, San Francisco: HarperSanFrancisco.

Drucker, Peter (1989), *The New Realities*, San Francisco: Harper & Row.

Eisler, Riane (1987), *The Chalice and the Blade*, San Francisco: Harper & Row (1995), *Sacred Pleasure: Sex, Myth and the Politics of the Body*, New York: HarperCollins.

Eliade, Mircea (1961), *The Sacred and the Profane*, San Francisco: Harper & Row. (1978), *A History of Religious Ideas*, 2 Vols., Chicago: University of Chicago Press.

Evola, Julius (1983), *The Metaphysics of Sex*, London: East-West Publications.

Ferguson, Kitty (1994), *The Fire in the Equations*, New York & London: Bantam.

Ferguson, Marilyn (1982), *The Aquarian Conspiracy: Personal and Social Transformation in the 1980s*, London: Routledge & Kegan Paul.

Fiand, Barbara (1987), *Releasement: Spirituality for Ministry*, New York: Crossroad.

Fowler, James (1981), *Stages of Faith*, San Francisco: Harper & Row. (1984), *Becoming Adult, Becoming Christian*, San Francisco: Harper & Row.

Fox, Matthew (1994), *The Reinvention of Work*, San Francisco: HarperSanFrancisco.

Fuellenbach, John (1995), *The Kingdom of God*, Maryknoll, NY: Orbis Books.

Garrett, Laurie (1995), *The Coming Plague: Newly Emerging Diseases in a World out of Balance*, London: Penguin Books.

Giddens, Anthony (1992), *The Transformation of Intimacy*, Oxford: Blackwell.

Gimbutas, Marija (1982), *The Goddesses and Gods of Old Europe, 7000-3500 BC*, Berkeley: University of California Press. (1991), *The Civilisation of the Goddess*, San Francisco: HarperSanFrancisco.

Gleick, James (1987), *Chaos: Making a New Science*, London: Heinemann.

Goldenberg, Naomi (1979), *Changing of the Gods*, Boston: Beacon Press.

Greenstein, George (1988), *The Symbiotic Universe*, New York: William Morrow & Co.

Guthrie, Stewart (1993), *Faces in the Clouds: A New Theory of Religion*, London: Oxford University Press.

Hampson, Daphne (1990), *Theology and Feminism*, Oxford: Blackwell.

Handy, Charles (1994), *The Empty Raincoat: Making Sense of the Future*, London: Hutchinson.

Harris, Maria (1991), *Dance of the Spirit: The Seven Steps of Women's Spirituality*, New York & London: Bantam Books.

Harrisville, Roy A. (1993), 'In Search of the Meaning of the Reign of God', *Interpretation*, Vol. 47, pp. 140–51.

Haught, John F. (1993), *The Promise of Nature: Ecology and Cosmic Purpose*, New York: Paulist Press.

Hay, David (1996), 'Religion Lacking Spirit', *The Tablet*, (2 March 1996), pp. 292–93.

Henderson, Hazel (1981), *The Politics of the Solar Age*, New York: Anchor Books.

Heyward, Carter (1988), *Our Passion for Justice*, New York: Pilgrim Press. (1989), *Touching our Strength: The Erotic as Power and the Love of God*, San Francisco: Harper.

Hillman, James (1985), *Anima: An Anatomy of a Personified Notion*, Irving, Texas: Spring Publications.

Hunt, Mary (1982), *Fierce Tenderness: A Feminist Theology of Friendship*, New York: Crossroad.

Jantsch, Erich (1980), *The Self-Organizing Universe*, Oxford: Pergamon Press.

Keen, Sam (1989), *Fire in the Belly*, London: Piatkus.

Kelly, Tony (1993), *An Expanding Theology: Faith in a World of Connections*, Sydney: E. J. Dwyer.

Kilpatrick, William (1975), *Intimacy and Identity*, New York: Delta Books.

King, Ursula (1989), *Women and Spirituality*, London: Macmillan. (1994), *Feminist Theology from the Third World*, New York: Orbis Books; London: SPCK.

Knitter, Paul F. (1995), *One Earth, Many Religions: Multifaith Dialogue & Global Responsibility*, Maryknoll: Orbis Books.

Kornfield, Jack (1993), *A Path With Heart: A Guide Through the Perils and Promises of Spiritual Life*, New York: Bantam.

Kuhn, Thomas (1970), *The Structure of Scientific Revolutions*, Chicago: University of Chicago Press.

Laszlo, Erwin (1993), *The Creative Cosmos*, Edinburgh: Floris Books.

Lawlor, Robert (1989), *Earth Honoring: The New Male Sexuality*, New York: Park St Press.

Leakey, Meave (1995), 'The Dawn of Humans,' *National Geographic*, 188 (Sept. 1995), pp. 38–51.

Leakey, Richard E. (1992), *Origins Reconsidered: In Search of What Makes us Human*, London: Abacus Books.

Leakey, Richard & Lewin, Roger (1996), *The Sixth Extinction*, London: Weidenfeld & Nicolson.

Leeming, David & Page, Jack (1994), *Goddess: Myths of the Female Divine*, Oxford: Oxford University Press.

Lewin, Roger (1993), *Complexity: Life at the Edge of Chaos*, London: J. M. Dent.

Lovelock, James (1979), *Gaia: A New Look at Life on Earth*, Oxford: Oxford University Press. (1988), *The Ages of Gaia*, Oxford: Oxford University Press.

Matthews, Caitlin (1991), *Sophia: Goddess of Wisdom*, New York: HarperCollins.

Matthews, Robert (1992), *Unravelling the Mind of God: Mysteries at the Frontier of Science*, London: Virgin Books.

McClintock-Fulkerson, Mary (1994), *Changing the Subject: Women's Discourses and Feminist Theology*, Minneapolis: Fortress Press.

McLean, Adam (1989), *Triple Goddess: An Exploration of the Archetypal Feminine*, Grand Rapids: Phanes.

Miller, David L. (1986), *Three faces of God: Traces of the Trinity in Literature and Life*, Philadelphia: Fortress Press.

Mithen, Steven (1996), *The Prehistory of the Mind*, London: Thames & Hudson.

Monick, E. (1987), *Phallos: Sacred Image of the Masculine*, Toronto: Inner City Books.

Moore, Robert & Gillete Douglas (1990), *King, Warrior, Magician, Lover*, San Francisco: Harper. (1993), *The Lover Within: Accessing the Lover in the Male Psyche*, New York: William Morrow & Co.

Moore, Thomas (1992), *Care of the Soul*, San Francisco: Harper; London: Piatkus (1994), *Soulmates*, San Francisco: Harper; Shrewsbury: Element.

Morgan, Robin (1989), *The Demon Lover: On the Sexuality of Terrorism*, London: Methuen.

Nelson, James B. & Longfellow, Sandra P. – Eds. (1994), *Sexuality and the Sacred: Sources for Theological Reflection*, Louisville, KY: Westminister/John Knox; London: Mowbrays

Nolan, Albert (1988), *God in South Africa: The Challenge of the Gospel*, Grand Rapids: Eerdmanns Publishing Co.

Nouwen, Henri (1986), *Reaching Out*, New York: Image Books.

Ó Murchú, Diarmuid (1992), *Our World in Transition*, London: Temple House Books. (1997), *Quantum Theology*, New York: Crossroad.

Pearson, Carol S. (1989), *The Hero Within: Six Archetypes We Live By*, San Francisco: HarperSanFrancisco.

Plaskow, Judith & Christ, Carol P. (1989), *Weaving The Visions: New Patterns in Feminist Spirituality*, New York: Harper & Row.

Riceour, Paul (1967), *The Symbolism of Evil*, Boston: Beacon Press. (1976), *Interpretation Theory: Discourse and the Surplus of Meaning*, Waco, TX: TCU Press. (1977), *The Rule of Metaphor*, Toronto: Toronto University Press.

Robertson, James (1986), *Future Work*, London: Gower.

Rolheiser, Ronald (1979), *The Restless Heart*, Denville, NJ: Dimension Books.

Ross, Susan A. & Hilkert, Mary Catherine (1995), 'Feminist Theology: A Review of Literature', *Theological Studies*, Vol. 56, pp. 327–52.

Ruether, Rosemary Radford (1985), *Women-Church: Theology and Practice of Feminist Liturgical Communities*, San Francisco: Harper & Row.

Russell, Letty M. (1981), *The Future of Partnership*, Philadelphia: John Knox Press. (1993), *Church in the Round*, Philadelphia: John Knox Press.

Russell, Robert John; Murphy, Nancey & Isham, C. J. (Eds) (1993), *Quantum Cosmology and the Laws of Nature*, Rome: Vatican Observatory Publications & Berkley (CA): The Centre for Theology and the Natural Sciences.

Sahtouris, Elisabet (1989), *Gaia: The Human Journey from Chaos to Cosmos*, London & New York: Pocket Books.

Saliba, John A. (1995), *Perspectives on New Religious Movements*, London: Chapman.

Schmidt, Roger (1980), *Exploring Religion*, London: Wadsworth.

Schneiders, Sandra (1991), *Beyond Patching*, New York: Paulist Press.

Schussler-Fiorenza, Elizabeth (1983), *In Memory of Her*, London: SCM Press.

Schwartz-Salan, Nathan & Stein, Murray (Eds) (1991), *Liminality and Transitional Phenomena*, Wilmette, Ill: Chiron Publications.

Sheehan, Thomas (1986), *The First Coming: How the Kingdom of God Became Christianity*, New York: Random House.

Sheldrake, Philip (1991), *Spirituality and History*, London: SPCK.

Singer, June (1977), *Androgyny: Toward a New Theory of Sexuality*, New York: Anchor Books.

Some, Malidoma Patrice (1993), *Ritual: Power, Healing and Community*, Portland, Or: Swan/Raven & Co.

Swimme, Brian & Berry, Thomas (1992), *The Universe Story*, San Francisco: Harper.

Tannahill, Reay (1980), *Sex in History*, London: Hamish Hamilton.

Taylor, Marc C. (1984), *Erring: A Post/modern A/theology*, Chicago: University of Chicago Press.

Trible, Phyliss (1978), *God and the Rhetoric of Sexuality*, Philadelphia: Fortress Press.

Verschuur, Gerritl (1978), *Cosmic Catastrophes*, London: Addison-Wesley.

Viviano, B. T. (1988), *The Kingdom of God in History*, Collegeville, Mn: Michael Glazier.

Waldrop M. Mitchell (1992), *Complexity: The Emerging Science at the Verge of Chaos*, New York: Viking.

Walker, Barbara G. (1990), *Women's Rituals: A Sourcebook*, San Francisco: Harper & Row.

Weeks, Jeffrey (1985), *Sexuality and its Discontents*, London: Routledge and Kegan Paul.

Wellwood, John (1991), *Journey of the Heart*, San Francisco: Harper.

Wheatley, Margaret J. (1992), *Leadership and the New Science*, San Francisco: Berrett-Koehler Publishers Inc.

Wilber, Ken (1996), *A Brief History of Everything*, Dublin: Gill & Macmillan; Boston: Shambhala.

Wilson, Edward O. (1992), *The Diversity of Life*, London: Penguin Books

Wyly, James (1989), *The Phallic Quest: Priapus and Masculine Inflation*, Toronto: Inner City Books.

Zappone, Katherine (1991), *The Hope for Wholeness: A Spirituality for Feminists*, Mystic (Conn): Twenty-Third Publs; Dublin: Columba Press.

Zohar, Danah (1991), *The Quantum Self*, London: Flamingo Books. (1993), *The Quantum Society*, London: Flamingo Books.

Index